False Idols

How Diversion is Destroying Democracy

Kurt Warner

Critical Perspectives on Social Science

VERNON PRESS

www.vernonpress.com

In the Americas:
Vernon Press
1000 N West Street, Suite 1200
Wilmington, Delaware, 19801
United States

In the rest of the world:
Vernon Press
C/Sancti Espiritu 17,
Malaga, 29006
Spain

Critical Perspectives on Social Science

Library of Congress Control Number: 2024946681

ISBN: 979-8-8819-0183-7

Also available: 979-8-8819-0084-7 [Hardback]; 979-8-8819-0182-0 [PDF, E-Book]

Cover design by Vernon Press with elements from Freepik.

Table of Contents

Table of Contents

To Tanya Warner and in memory of Elissa Warner, with love

Foreword

Dr. Bryan Flynn
Binghamton University

Nearly 20 years ago, I began my career in higher education. In that time, I have had the pleasure of teaching, advising and admitting hundreds of students in a role I often considered to be a gatekeeper to the profession of social work. Ultimately, my commitment was and continues to be to the thousands of clients my students would end up serving throughout their careers. Being in a position to help guide students through their journey of becoming compassionate and effective practitioners and one that comes with a great deal of responsibility and joy.

The joy comes from working with and getting to know students like the author of this book. Kurt is the kind of student instructors love to have in class and the kind of student graduate directors love to have as a representative of their program. Not only is he academically gifted, but he is also kind and empathetic. Kurt will be a lifelong learner and he was one of our finest students and he is now a colleague and friend. When you read his book, you will undoubtedly agree that he is highly committed to the well-being of the clients he serves and to issues of social justice and individual and societal ethical integrity.

My experiences as a clinician have taken me to Ground Zero following the terrorist attacks on 9/11, providing end-of-life care to patients in an HIV clinic and to a trauma center emergency room meeting the non-medical needs of patients and their families. Throughout my career, I have worked with people facing traumatic loss, chronic illness, psychiatric emergencies and addiction. Today, I work with first responders and veterans who are working to unpack years of accumulated trauma.

This book is about distraction and how distraction often takes us off the path of what is important. As a social worker, I often help my clients identify the distractions in their lives so that they can prioritize and focus on what is truly important to them. There are the external distractions in our lives, many of which Kurt covers here so eloquently, but also there are the internal distractions and these are often the emotions and feelings that set us off on paths we were not planning or hoping to go down. Anger, fear and sadness, when left unchecked, permeate our relationships, our communication patterns, our motivation, our hopes and aspirations, and of course, our physical well-being. The "big 3", as I like to think of them, are the main rivers of emotion (along with love and joy but typically people do not seek out the help of a therapist when they are feeling happy or are in love). The big 3 can leave us feeling lost, isolated, confused and hopeless. The feelings that often (hopefully) lead someone to seek out help. Anger, fear, and sadness are rivers that contain our depression about the past and our anxiety about the future. Out of those rivers, flow tributaries that lead to feelings like frustration, envy, regret, resentment and worry. These things distract us. They cause alienation in our relationships. They cost us jobs and other opportunities by playing on our insecurities and other cognitive distortions. They make us retreat from the world and they distract us from working through what is often at the root of our pain, which is usually grief. Grief is not just about the loss of a loved one. We also grieve the loss of control, identity, belonging, community, purpose, safety, desire and goals. But most of us do not talk openly about that grief. Many of us are taught – particularly men – both implicitly and explicitly that anger, which is the gatekeeper to grief, is acceptable to demonstrate and express openly. But not grief. Grief many of us are not sure what to do with. We avoid talking openly about it. When we see people we love grieving, we try to distract and hope that it goes away quickly and on its own. Anger and fear are at the very accessible surface of our emotional selves. Grief is at the base and most significant level of our pain. And when we are not allowed to process it, to talk openly about it, we are distracted from working through it. Grief is a difficult enough road to travel down but when it is complicated by the distractions in our lives, it impedes our ability to find acceptance, empathy, gratitude and forgiveness.

As evidenced, anger, fear, sadness, and the many emotional tributaries that flow from them can be personally destructive and serve as distractions to the individual, deterring us from confronting grief, the root of our pain, and distracting us from pursuing a better life. In a similar way, Kurt illustrates how the external distractions from the larger systems of society can be collectively destructive and take us off course from confronting our civic duty and engaging in the greater good. It is only through the recognition of these external distractions that we can stop being led astray from them and instead engage in and enhance our democracy. In this book, Kurt helps us identify the distractions that deter us from contributing to the betterment of the collective whole. He paves the way for us. He provides here what we need to do to set our compass in the direction and path in which we want to travel. It is up to us not to get distracted.

Preface

Rome was a great empire. The United States is a great Empire. Rome was born out of a great story. The United States was born out of a great story. Rome had a variety of tragic flaws. The United States has a variety of tragic flaws. Rome dissolved and devolved due to those flaws. The United States is devolving and dissolving due to those flaws.

The Roman Empire was founded around 753 B.C. This was when Romulus and Remus established the city that would become the empire: Rome. It started as a monarchy but became a "Republic" in 509 B.C. The power of the monarchy was transferred into elected consuls or magistrates. These magistrates, while 'elected,' were most often drawn from Rome's Senate, which was wholly made up of the patrician, or rich class. This created a class formation in ancient Rome between patrician (rich) and plebeian (poor). (Rodgers, 2016).

Does this sound familiar?

In other words, Rome was a dictatorship in its infancy... for over two hundred years. Then, class warfare and the economic and social forces inevitably forced it to change into a Republic, which gave some power to the people, or at least gave the illusion of power to the people. But that power was only *superficial*. The wealthy patricians made sure to pull all the strings in the new "Republic," or representative, form of government and wrested control of the Republic from the people by maintaining the power over the Senate. The Senate was, in name, there to represent the people. (Rodgers, 2016) However, most of those 'elected' to it were likely almost entirely incredibly rich and arrogant people who cared more about their massive house and how many servants they had than about the welfare of the people they represented.

One can only imagine how marginalized the Roman people and, especially, the plebian, or common person, were throughout these years in the Roman Republic.

In around 100 A.D., the Roman poet Juvenal wrote, in *Satire* 10, 77-81,

> *Already long ago, from when we sold our vote to no man, the People have abdicated our duties; for the People who once upon a time handed out military command, high civil office, legions — everything, now restrains itself and anxiously hopes for just two things: bread and circuses.*

This line is amongst the most poignant and thought-provoking in Roman literature and perhaps even in human history. He chastises the masses, the plebeians, for falling short of their civic duties. He commends what they once did but states that they are now complacent if they have two things: bread and circuses. "Bread and circuses" refers to physiological needs and entertainment (PBS.org, 2006). In other words, Juvenal states that the people have been pacified by chasing their basic needs and fun. He says that this fun and physiological satiation blinds them to their duty to maintain society. The pacification caused by these "bread and circuses" creates apathy to the civic duties that create a functioning republic or democracy. Because everyone is distracted by "bread and circuses," no one is doing what is necessary to be doing to save the country.

At this point, this story *has* to sound familiar.

Rome lasted about a thousand years. The United States has recently logged its two-hundred-and-forty-seventh birthday. Despite having many, many tools the Romans didn't (such as the benefit of history), the United States has arrived at a very similar negative state of affairs in record time. There are plenty of variables along the way that could have served as a catalyst for this metamorphosis to occur quicker. But we are here nonetheless.

Many historians have discussed the decline of Rome and the fact that this decline was not necessary. Historian Edward Watts (2020), in *How Rome Fell into Tyranny,* said that Rome traded freedom and a Republican government for tyranny and an autocratic government. This occurred due to Roman leaders manipulating the rules and pursuing selfish gain rather than looking for the well-being of the people. They usurped power, used red herrings to occupy the people's interest, and created civil wars. Does this sound familiar?

In, *The History and Fall of the Roman Empire,* historian Edward Gibbon (1999) wrote a massive, six-volume work on Rome. What was his thesis? He argued that a gradual abandonment of *civic duty* by the Roman people enabled barbaric tribes around Rome to come in and invade successfully. Does the abandonment of civic duty sound familiar?

The Western Roman Empire was destroyed by barbarian invasions (Editors of the Encyclopedia Britannica, 2024). Within the walls of Rome, there were economic troubles and fights that kept the Romans in a constant state of anxiety. The greed that caused the gap between the rich and the poor was overwhelming. The rich often fled their tax obligations by setting up independent fiefdoms in the countryside outside of Rome. Rome depended on cheap slave labor that enriched the wealthy and insured the poor had fewer opportunities. All of this inner turmoil made its outer shell very weak and easy to conquer by barbaric tribes. (Rodgers, 2016) Does this polarization of wealth and the rich putting their creation of wealth (outsourcing, tax breaks) ahead of the welfare of the country sound familiar?

Another factor that caused Rome's fall was the tremendous division between Eastern and Western Empire (Editors of the Encyclopedia Britannica, 2024). This obviously created tremendous challenges for the Empire as it divided the Roman people into halves. As Lincoln (1953) said, "A house divided against itself cannot stand" (p. 147). This division created a house that could no longer stand. Does the polarization of parties and peoples in a country at a record pace sound like something you've heard before?

Rome performed excellently in its infancy. However, government corruption was likely common in any empire as vast as Rome. For many centuries, it was minimal. But after the corruption began, it grew widely. It got so bad that even being emperor was entering into a death sentence. For example, between 235 CE to 285 CE, 33 Roman Emperors were either murdered or executed (Cilliers & Retief, 2010). The anger and antagonism they experienced clearly made governing impossible. Do calls for the assassination of prominent political leaders sound familiar? Think 2021.

The Roman Empire remains today the longest standing by some metrics greatest empires in all of human history. A great many complex variables created divisions that led to its fall. This brief overview is given to make clear that the fall of Rome from the inside is what made it possible to destroy Rome from the outside. In other words, Rome rotted, withered, and died on the inside long before it was left vulnerable for the scavengers to destroy it from the outside. Juvenal was writing his wise words as Rome had begun its dissent and its rot, internally.

Now, let's examine Rome's parallels to the present-day United States.

The United States does not always seem to be an overly popular actor on the world stage. Many countries in the world have animosity toward the United States, and it appears that many may not wish the United States well. The recent effort of China to align with Russia in the midst of Russia's war against Ukraine may be an illustration of this. I make this analogy because while we no longer have tribes who invade other tribes, we do have alliances between countries against other countries. To illustrate the severity of this parallel, in the last year of Donald Trump's presidency, in a Gallup survey published on January 15, 2021, across sixty countries and areas, median approval of his leadership was a mere 22%, and the highest rating he received from these countries was a mere 33% (Ray, J., 2021). The United States is very much like Rome even in that we are perceived negatively which seems to be a clear indication of its withering strength externally.

As noted, the United States is, as Lincoln said, "a house divided against itself." Unlike the Romans, the internal division in the United States is not East and West. Rather, the internal division of the United States has always been north and south geographically and right and left ideologically. It has been divided since the 1860s, but in 2017, this division has grown to epic proportions. This also mimics Rome very strongly. Americans are no longer willing to hear each other out or amicably resolve their differences. As USC News has noted, the United States has become politically and socially polarized in a way that has not been seen since the Civil War. (Paisley, 2016).

Both the internal and external divisions that the United States has are often fanned by the corruption in its politics. Corruption has always had a place in American politics. The corruption of politics may lead to the practice of buying and selling offices with the money that seems to control politics on all levels. This aristocracy and love of wealth dominated and corrupted Roman politics in a very similar way. It sowed the seeds of division and created a manipulation by the upper classes of the lower classes, just as in America. (Perkins, 2020).

These divisions are being manipulated by the leaders of the United States. This manipulation is causing mobs based on erroneous ideologies to form. These mobs are threatening and attacking American leaders in a way that they, like Roman leaders, fear for their lives. Nancy Pelosi, whose husband, Paul, was attacked by an assailant who was trying to kill or hurt her, demonstrated senseless mob violence based on an erroneous ideology. The list of hate and violence toward American elected representatives has always been a feature in the United States (Suri, 2022). However, it seems to have accelerated greatly since 2020. The most obvious and glaring example of American political violence was when Trump's supporters stormed the capital and murdered a capital policeman in an attempt to seize the capital and kill Democratic lawmakers all in an attempt for him to retain his power. These divisions are rendering our efforts to create a reasonable society wherein we treat each other humanely almost impossible. These are the battles within that weaken us as just ancient Rome was weakened.

The United States is weakened by its wealth in the same way that Rome was weakened by theirs. Whereas the Roman wealthy set up fiefdoms outside of Rome so as to avoid their taxes, American corporations do the same in the same way at a record rate. While Rome depended on cheap, slave labor imported from outside lands to do its bidding and to make the rich richer, the United States has policies that enable corporations to find cheaper slave labor in other countries to make American products rather than employ Americans. All of this, like in Rome, serves to make the rich richer and to create an incredibly polarized society. In both Rome and America, disparities in wealth created virtual economic caste systems.

As you can see, there are plenty of parallels between Rome and the United States. This book will be focusing on one parallel in particular. Juvenal's "Bread and circuses" are today's "basic necessities and distractions." As long as we stay distracted by engaging in what doesn't matter, those in power will be free to enrich themselves and engage in what does matter for us. If we can see this diversion, which Cambridge Advanced Learner's Dictionary (2023) defines as, "something that takes your attention away from something else," we can stop it. That is the hope of this book. It is to ask you to choose what idol you find meaningful for your life, rather than allowing society and its motives to thrust its false idols upon you. It is the hope that we can stop worshiping the false idols of money, of entertainment, of distracting ourselves with the meaningless and to learn to engage in the meaningful. It is a clarion call to shake free of the shackles of our collective daze and wake up and embrace what the Romans held above all since the times of Virgil – duty. Because it is in duty, and duty alone, that we can stop being made complacent by the "bread and circuses" of our lives and start resurrecting the greatness of our existence. Duty could help relieve us of the false idols we have come to spend so much of our time trying to emulate and looking up to as if they were greater than ourselves.

This book will examine those false idols in many aspects of contemporary life. We will see how celebrities are ready-made idols by profit-driven places with motives. We will see how the culture creates false idols for us to adore and how, by indulging these idols, we abrogate our responsibility to each other and to the greater community. It will discuss how sports target a different audience but effectively serve the same purpose. It will discuss the concept of hegemony and how it is alive and well. It will show how politicians and the political sphere use their own system of false idols or "bread and circuses" to keep us thinking about and occupied with anything but what matters. It will examine how art, music, and literature reflect society but also are often being used as manipulation that creates a false sense of security and distraction. It will examine the Internet, video games, and other devices to show how they, too, come together to pacify the masses and keep them in check with the "bread and circuses" that they can provide.

Finally, the book will discuss the concept of sobering ourselves from the opiate of false idols. It examines our thought processes and how the aggregate effects of all of these false idols are to shape our thoughts and desensitize us to ourselves. It asks us to consistently examine the way we live and wake up from the collective daze that has fallen on society. It explores the concept of change. It asks us what change could look like in a society so drugged by the onslaught of images and distractions that keep us from focusing on the things that matter. Whether we are talking about the crumbling of the republic in ancient Rome or the decay of democracy in America, one truth remains static. We created the systems and we created the structure. If we create it, we can change it. So, let's explore our false idols.

Introduction

Chris is a thirty-nine-year-old appliance salesman. He lives in Syracuse, New York and has spent most of his life there. He has a wife named Joelle, and she works as a reporter for the local television station. They have a child, Dominic, who is 10 years old. Both Chris and Joelle work very hard to support the ten-year-old son and provide both the emotional resources and the economic resources that are needed to create the quality of life that they want for him. They also work very hard to provide the emotional and economic resources that they want to create their own life.

Chris wakes up at seven in the morning and shakes the fatigue from his brain. He immediately grabs his phone, which sits next to him and functions as his alarm clock on his nightstand. He opens his calendar app. His eyes are immediately drawn to the large and animated advertisement for the newest razor that he could use for that "extra close shave" that will obviously improve his life. He looks at the advertisement and recognizes the celebrity who is attesting to the quality of the razor ever so briefly by shaving in one fluid motion. Chris then taps the day and views what obligations he has put in for the day.

"Good morning, honey," he says to his wife who is awake an hour before him to get ready for her job.

"Good morning dear," she says with her face contorted as she's putting on her mascara. "Dominic is eating his breakfast now, and there should be a little bit left over if you want some."

"Sounds good," Chris says, and as he says this, he hears the television in the living room.

"Make your wife happy with Dr. Tom's deodorant. It will last all day and make the people around you stay," are the first words he hears other than his wife's for that day. He pays no attention to the advertisement, but he heard it. He walks over to the dining room table where his son sits and eagerly chomps on a dark and chocolatey-looking cereal. His son holds the spoon as if it were a shovel and spoons spoonful after spoonful into his mouth. Chris sees the very large and brown box of "Chocolate Puffs" which includes a picture of the cereal as well as a picture of several animated chocolate-based characters that are extremely happy and inviting.

"How's my favorite little buddy this morning?" Chris asks.

"Good," Dominic says with a full mouth and does not look up at his dad. Rather, he seems overly fixated on his phone as he navigates his social media sites and a wide variety of apps that have all the same advertisements and more. Chris moves on and starts to move toward the kitchen when his son states,

"Can I get the new Mokata VN smartphone?" he asked his dad. "Jeff has it, and it has better apps and newer features that I really need, Dad. Everything that I'm seeing from the commercial said that I will be able to do better in school if I get it. Can I have it? Please?"

Chris looked overwhelmed by the question. He turned to his son and wiped the sweat off his brow due to the warmth in the apartment. "We'll see," he said to his son. "Right now, I'm looking to wake up and get a little breakfast. We can talk about the possibility of getting a new phone later."

Chris continued his walk into the kitchen, and his eyes glazed over the "Winza" emblem on the stove, the "Arcada" microwave logo, the "Foodmaster" refrigerator logo, and others as he stepped into the room. He did not consciously see any of these things, but he did see them, and they resided in his unconscious mind the rest of the day and every day.

He opened the refrigerator and saw Baro's Cola cans, several quarts of Aunt Mina's Orange Juice, Johnson's soy milk carton, and an onslaught of other company names that are written on every food that he owned. He paid no attention to any of these and reached automatically for the orange juice. He walked over to the counter, filled a glass full of orange juice, and walked over to the chair next to his son. He saw at the table where there was oatmeal in a bowl and toast on a dish.

"How come you're not eating any of mom's oatmeal or toast?"

It took about thirty seconds for Dominic to stop chewing his chocolate puffs. "Because they are boring. Everybody else eats chocolate puffs or cereal like it."

"Well, why do you want to be like everybody else?"

Dominic responded instantly, "Nobody likes the guy who is left out, dad," he said and shook his head as if this was obvious.

Chris got himself a bowl of oatmeal as he sat next to his son. The ladle that he had to use to put his oatmeal into his bowl read, "Kitchen-Haven." He made no notice of it and continued to prepare and eat his food.

As Chris and his son sat ate breakfast, "American Titan Ninja" was on the television in front of them. Chris simply sat next to his son and ate his oatmeal and watched the show.

There were almost as many commercial breaks as there was show on "American Titan Ninja." During one of the many commercial breaks, Chris watched an ad for the Mokata VN smartphone. It featured extremely upbeat music and many happy people using Mokata smartphones to engage in all kinds of activities. The colors in the commercial were vibrant and lively and happy. There was a constant flow of text at the bottom of the commercial that listed all kinds of things the phone can do. Near the end of the commercial, the text read, "It will help you get better grades."

"You see! Did you see it?" Dominic said excitedly to his dad. "I'll do better in school if you get me the phone! So you have to get it, dad!"

"Yes, I see it Dom," Chris said softly to his son. "We'll see about it. I'm not making any promises because we just bought that phone a few months ago."

Dominic was unhappy with this response. "That's just it, dad, you bought it for me a few months ago! Now it's an outdated piece of junk," he said with disgust as he pushed the phone across the table. "I need *that* phone now."

Chris shook his head at his son. "We'll see, buddy. I've got to get to work."

Dominic looked visibly disappointed. He pulled his phone back toward him and resumed his activity on social media as he shoveled more chocolate puffs into his mouth.

Chris continued to eat his food, and as he finished, he got up and went into the bathroom.

His wife, Joelle, was just finishing up her makeup and was walking out of the bathroom.

"Can you pick him up after school today? Joelle asked.

"Of course." The two kissed each other, and Joelle walked into the living room, spoke to her son, and left. Chris took a shower, got ready for the day, and walked Dominic to the bus stop where he could get a ride to school. After that, he walked to the parking garage, where he kept his car. As he walked up to his car, he saw the "Bard Motors" emblem before he got into it.

Chris listened to the radio as he drove to work. He liked to listen to the news and as he listened to the news, one out of every three minutes was filled by a commercial.

"The last things you need to worry about are your credit card bills. There are entities out there that are willing to settle your debt for a fraction of what you owe. Isn't it time for you to get rid of your debt? Call us, and we will get rid of it for you."

"Have you or your loved one struggled with addiction? You don't have to live this way. We have medications that will stop your addiction and allow you to live a life free of substance use. We have worked with people throughout the state and throughout the country. And we could save you from your chemical dependency. Just call us."

"Are you miserable at your job? Are you looking for something different? Remark Corporation has a job for you. We'll pay you a fair wage and we will put you in a work atmosphere that keeps you healthy. Go to our website and apply today and watch as your life transforms."

"Do you love your family? Then buy them the best. Come into your local Hailstrom store where we have all of what you need. Shop for him, her, your kids or anyone else. Hailstorm has something for everyone and we're selling everything at 50% off. Plus, we'll give you one of our coupons for even more savings! Come in today and we'll share the love with you!"

And finally,

"Hey, friends, are you eating the best foods? If you're not, come into Natalie's Organic Supermarket. We are featuring organic foods to fit your needs, including freshly sliced fruits and vegetables from farms right out of our state. Feed your family the best. Feed them Natalie's Organic Supermarket."

This was the first round of commercials that Chris did not listen to but he heard before he even got to the stop sign in his development. By the time he arrived at his appliance shop, he would hear a different version of those commercials three more times.

As he drove through the fresh spring air of Syracuse, he kept his window down and the wind whipped through his car and tousled his hair. He was into a political show that told him how he should vote, think about issues, and conceive of his relationship with his wife and children. As he sat at a red light in the city, his eyes were drawn to many billboards that lined the streets in the city and throughout the area.

One billboard featured a beautiful woman drinking out of a coconut and stated that he could, "Trade rush hour for happy hour by signing on with Funsies Vacations." The woman was in a bathing suit and relaxing on a beach and drinking out of the coconut with a straw that was blatantly suggestive.

Another billboard featured a perfect-looking soft drink: a cola bubbling over with ice frosting the glass with the straw sticking out of it. The text next to it read, "Tastes like a million dollars. Only costs one." It featured the colors yellow and orange, which are subliminally known to create hunger.

Still, another billboard featured a handsome and rugged man with a cigarette in his mouth as he posed for the camera by looking off into the distance. It had an inscription next to his visage stating, "Bold taste. Smooth Flavor. Markett Cigarettes."

Between his cell phone, his television, his radio, and his drive to work, Chris encountered more than two thousand ads before noon. By the end of the day, he would see, hear, or be exposed to just short of 10,000 ads. According to a Forbes magazine article in 2017 entitled, "Finding Brand Success in the Digital World," most Americans are exposed to between 4,000 to 10,000 ads each day (Simpson, 2017). This constant deluge of corporate coercion serves to divert us from ourselves and from the reality around us. These ads tell us how we should think, what we should do, where we should go, and who we are. The herd instinct does the rest. We follow the crowd and feel intense social pressure to abide by the will of the herd. When we abide by the will of the herd, we give up our autonomy of will and our freedom of thought. When we give up our autonomy of will and our freedom of thought, we become docile and subject to manipulation by our leaders, both corporate and political.

Therefore, advertising is just one of the many false idols that we have come to worship in our society. It is one form of the "bread and circuses" that we are given to occupy our minds and consume our activity. None of us ever think about the fact that we are seeing anywhere from 4,000 to 10,000 advertisements each and every day. But we are. And it is never said on the newscast or in any ad. What is left unsaid is often what is most important to hear. This book attempts to bring these seemingly endless efforts to divert our attention to what doesn't matter to light. Because it is only by seeing and recognizing what doesn't matter, that we can come to see and recognize what does.

Chapter 1

Wake Up

The term idol, according to Collins dictionary (2023), means "a statute or other object that is worshiped by people who believe it is a god" (para. 2). Anything that is worshiped or given endless attention and looked up to as if it is something greater than oneself can qualify as an idol. Idols are common and the traditional definition for idol by Merriam-Webster dictionary is, "an object of extreme devotion" (para. 1). Idols, then, are individuals or entities to which we devote ourselves so zealously that they can become deified on some level.

Idolatry, according to the American Heritage Dictionary (2000), is, "the worship of idols" (para. 1). Put more clearly, idolatry is, then, the worship of a statue or object by people who believe it is a god. Therefore, any false idol is something that we devote ourselves to worship in a way that mimics that devotion that would traditionally be reserved for a higher power.

The concept of idolatry is derived from the ancient world and probably existed as long as human beings have existed. The concept has played a pivotal role in the history of Western religious ideology. Daniel Barbu argues that from the origin of the term idolatry, it was used to mean 'false religion.' He goes on to state that the category of idolatry emerged at the intersection of Judaism and early Greek Christianity (Barbu, 2022).

There are an almost endless amount of passages that can be discussed to exhibit the concept of idolatry in at least three of the world's major religions. However, this is being presented simply to know the history of the concept and to suggest that the concepts of the ancient world, despite all of the technological progress and the massive amount of human ingenuity and invention that has occurred since then, continue to be the concepts that pervade the consciousness of the modern world.

Idolatry was generally and historically the worship of another god. However, in contemporary society, this worship has found many other outlets, and idolatry is being redefined. This new definition is based on the same endless search for meaning. The void in ourselves and the deeper desire we have to make sense of our existence is increasingly being filled with new and foreign idolatry. It is an idolatry that is almost wholly composed of vanity in its many, many forms.

In ancient Greek myth, the story of Narcissus was relayed by the ancient Greek author Ovid in his *Metamorphosis*. Narcissus was very attractive and was loved by everyone, but Narcissus never returned that love to anyone else. One day, a beautiful nymph, Echo, tried to hold him, but he scorned her as he scorned others. Because Narcissus scorned everyone who tried to love him, the gods made it so Narcissus could never have anything that he loved. One day, when Narcissus bent down to drink some water, he saw his own image. In that moment, he saw his own reflection, and became utterly infatuated with none other than himself. He stood and looked in the reflection and tried to grab it and did not eat or drink but stood utterly mesmerized by it. He stood and swore that he would not leave until he could be with the one he loved: the one he saw in the water reflected before him. He stayed and stared and wasted away until he died.

Narcissus worshipped at the altar of himself. He is the definition of vanity and Ovid presented us with an excellent cautionary tale. He wrote this around 8 A.D. At the time of this writing, it is currently 2024 A.D. However, the lessons of Narcissus continue to not be learned. Nourished by the self-interest that capitalism endlessly promotes, many of us are becoming Narcissus. Our economic system and the worldview that grows out of it have created a vanity and self-love the likes of which only Narcissus could understand.

In our endless quest for meaning in what may seem like a meaningless life, we have created and surrounded ourselves with false idols. Many of them are entities that we create outside of ourselves. Many of those are detailed in this book, and they are immensely dangerous to our society and work culture, to our humanity and to our morality. However, perhaps the most insidious form of idolatry is vanity. It is created by self-interest, and the only time a vain person is not looking inward is when their vanity is propelling them to compare themselves to what is outward in order to feel superior to it. A truly vain person has an intrinsically inverse relationship to hearing or loving anything outside of themselves because they are often so preoccupied with the adoration of themselves. As we become less democratic and more infatuated and obsessed with demigods of our own creation, we are becoming more distanced and isolated from each other. Our humanity is the opportunity cost of our vanity.

In the end, the false idols, that is, the "bread and circuses" and the endless pursuit of vanity create a world in which we are drifting apart rather than getting closer together. As Sophia Nelson, an award-winning journalist and author, states, "We are all frustrated with the culture of "cut off." The culture of "hiding" and "cyberbullying." Nobody talks anymore. Nobody listens anymore. We have allowed these gadgets, phones, and devices to ruin our ability to be intimate, vulnerable, and connected as people. The gadgets own us and not the other way around. This age of "social media connection" is causing division in families, in churches, in marriages, and friendships" (Nelson, 2014, para. 5).

This division is allowing us to lose everything we've gained. What is the point of having technology that enables us to talk to people all over the world if we can't hold a conversation with the person sitting next to us? What is the point of being able to visit the moon when we can't figure out how to create an equitable society on the celestial body we have? What is the point of endlessly distracting ourselves with whatever the herd is interested in when we never stop and take time to actually live the examined life that Socrates discussed, which enables and empowers us to understand ourselves and what we want out of that life?

Human beings have likely always chased false idols. It is important to remember that the concept of false idols is inherently based on psychological dependency. It suggests that we must be dependent upon something else for our needs and desires. Many of us find the dependence on God or another transcendent figure is not, in itself, harmful or dubious in any way. There is such a thing as healthy idols. The dependence that exists on those healthy idols is typically one that creates strength. For instance, if you believe in God and that God is with you and is watching and helping you navigate your existence, this can inspire you to transcend the problems that you have. There is a level of dependency, but it is a healthy dependency because it hurts no one. However, the moment that someone depends on a false idol that asks them to do something that is against basic and decent behavior and thought, the idol becomes a false one and is deleterious to one's moral, spiritual, and carnal being.

This is undoubtedly natural and a part of human existence. However, the concept that our quest should stall and linger based on the choice of these false idols is anathema to our existences. The continuing and current state of those who have learned to manipulate the masses with "bread and circuses" does not need to be a continuing part of our narrative. We can reframe and change our story.

Critic Gustav Freytag analyzed the structure of a typical five-act play and deconstructs the structure of a dramatic narrative art in a way that helps us understand it. Many reading this are likely familiar with part of his conceptualization: the rising action, climax, and falling action that occur in almost any narrative. (Penguin Dictionary, 1999) This has been used often in literature classes all over the world to understand the basic structure of a dramatic work.

His insight can provide guidance for our story. Yes, we have fallen into worshiping false idols. Yes, the hegemony of the ruling classes uses "bread and circuses" of all forms to distract and detach us from our own lives to continue their power. However, what if we just considered this the rising action to the human story? There have been many, many conflicts in battles in between, but the story tends to continue to repeat itself, much like George Santayana forecasted about history, when he said, "Those who cannot remember the past are condemned to repeat it" (Santayana, 1905).

However, what if we can stop repeating it? What if all of those back and forths throughout history, all of those battles between two forces, were just the rising action in the human narrative? What if all of it was just preparing us for one large climax that builds on the many small climaxes in the past? There is a path for us to take if we want it. It can rid us of having to ceaselessly relive and revisit the false idols and the many mistakes of the past.

That is why the title of this chapter is "Wake up." The phrase was taken from both Jim Morrison and Jack Kerouac, who each used it in their music and literature, respectively. Both argued for a reawakening of human consciousness, and both used their medium to present that reawakening to the public. Art, in all its many beautiful forms, is and always has been one of the greatest mediums to create social change. It is a canvas upon which messages can connect and resonate with other human beings. Both artists argued, on some level, implicitly sometimes and explicitly other times, for the creation of change in our existence. Both artists argued for us to "wake up" from the circumstances they were in, shake the cobwebs from our consciousness, and make positive changes in the world around us.

So, too, must we wake up. By waking up, we can realize the imprisonment that we experience from not only the hegemony of the outside world, but to the shackles of our inside world – our consciousness. The self-interested puppeteers that control the strings of our existence by pulling our consciousness in this direction and that direction with the products they make and avaricious desires that they have must be stopped. We've allowed these puppeteers to be created and we also have the power to banish them into the greedy darkness from where they came. We have the power to change the verbiage and structure of our leaders because we were the ones who elected them in the first place. We have the power to change the advertising structure that hooks us like fish by manipulating our weaknesses and desires and needs based on the psychological frailties that were created by society. We have the power to make sure the Internet does not continue to be co-opted by the greedy and the wealthy who want it to become and are quickly making it just another marketing tool and from those who are filling it with misinformation that misleads and confuses us as to what is truth and what is not. We have the power to let art in all its forms as music, literature, poetry, etc. to remain free and not constrained by the capitalistic desires of the individuals who serve as the gatekeepers to public consumption. We have the power to ensure that the economic system serves us and that we don't have to serve the economic system. We can create the system and make it right so that equity and fairness reign rather than division, greed, and exclusion.

What tools do we have? How can we remove our chains and break free of the shackles of that which we endure? This has a cultural answer. Culture is and remains one of the most powerful, if not the most powerful forces, that exists in regard to human behavior. L.S. Vygotsky, the founder of sociocultural theory and a Russian psychologist, suggested that learning occurs in social and cultural interaction (Allman, 2022).

Culture, then, is a teacher. If culture is changed, society will change. Therefore, a reexamination of values must occur and permeate culture for change to occur. For evidence of this, just look at the impact that Elvis had on the culture of the 1950s. One charismatic figure changed everything. You can see this in every country in one way or another. Mostly, every dictator started by creating a charismatic presence that "solved" some perceived problem or scapegoat. Through the manipulation of the masses by scapegoating, the culture went through tremendous change in every country where this has occurred.

However, in almost every case where culture changed due to a charismatic leader, the culture became morally bankrupt. This is not the answer. It replaces one influential figure with another in hopes that the new influential figure does not create an immoral existence for the people. In the end, the power for cultural change begins and ends in the hearts and minds of the individual.

This is why the answer is unequivocally connected to critical thinking. No wayward but charismatic leader can succeed in a democracy without the people's consent. No culture can fall into a herd-like state of acquiescence to false idols if the people can think for themselves. Therefore, critical thinking must be the revolution. This is the only way for true amelioration in a society that has grown bigger and more pregnant with problems than ever expected.

That's why there inevitably must be a revolt. Revolution is always necessary to make a change when the individuals who have the power to make the change are unwilling to make it. This conflict, this revolution, is native to almost every kind of meaningful change that has occurred on a societal level. It is good, moral, and just to rebel against unjust circumstances. This is how the United States was created, this is how civil rights were wrestled away from the individuals who held the power to withhold those civil rights, this is how Jesus resisted the Jewish and Roman governments, this is how Gandhi liberated India from the avarice of the English, and the list keeps going.

The means of revolution is the moral dilemma. The revolutionary has a wide range of choice regarding the means by which they revolt. Revolution never has to be violent. Revolution never has to be hateful. Revolution is generally defined as a forced overthrow of the system of government. However, the question of force is seldom defined. In the Revolutionary War, force consisted of guns and bayonets and one person's will against another. However, Jesus or Martin Luther King or Gandhi did not fire a single gun or drop a single bomb, and their means of revolution were every bit as effective. In fact, their revolutions were more effective because they changed the minds and hearts of those who they overthrew rather than physically forcing their dictators to change.

Albert Camus, in his essay *The Rebel* (1951), argues that when individuals are disenfranchised by the world around them, they should rebel. In other words, when there is a basic contradiction between what our minds perceive as reasonable and the absurdity of the constructs in the external world, rebellion becomes necessary. The concept of false idols that occupy the majority of our lives, leading us down a path of aimless vanity, is endless, pointless, and lends itself to rebellion. The concept of "bread and circuses," which continually distracts us from changing the system and creating the existence we want, creates complacency, apathy, and lends itself to rebellion. This rebellion is not against human beings but against ideas. It is not against each other but against the ideologies that have been allowed to be forced down our throats and that keep us paralyzed with indecision and angst.

The revolution, then, is a peaceful one. It is a revolution of thought. It is a return and devotion to critical thinking and creating new neuronal thought patterns that can free us of the chains of our existence. If we all put down the false idols and ignore the "bread and circuses," there will be a nonviolent revolt. This nonviolent revolt will inherently change the system that serves as a puppeteer controlling and pulling all of the strings of our false idols and endless supply of "bread and circuses." It is this rejection of norms and values that can free us and create a truly more perfect union wherein we can all share ourselves with each other in a caring way rather than fight, compete, and tear each other apart in a hateful way.

Plato recognized over two thousand years ago that a philosopher king was the best-suited leader of the society. In other words, a thinking leader is the strongest bulwark that a society has against the suffering of its citizens. However, a philosopher leader is not enough. We have the means of information and knowledge to create a philosopher people. This is the truest safeguard against our destruction and pain. Educated societies are societies devoid of false idols.

If there is no revolt, the erosion will continue. All that is true and good that we have developed and built in the thousands of years of our existence will cease to exist. We will remain the puppeteers to our political and economic systems, beholden to our politicians and our giant corporate masters, and we will be stuck in the endless pit, that is, the needless ditch of our own digging. There is a way out. It is for us to realize the power that we have. Unlike any animal which remains subservient to a human being because it does not know its strength, we must learn ours. It is not simply the power of the many, but it is the power of the mind. This is the power that human beings have had since the dawn of their existence. It is our superior mind, and not our superior muscle, that has always enabled us to succeed in previous times. If we can reevaluate our values and challenge our mindless norms and the strength of our mind, we can stop worshiping false idols. We can stop filling the meaningless void of our existence with what "bread and circuses" we are goaded to follow. We can build the world we want if we can only stop being distracted from and start thinking about what matters.

Chapter 2

Celebrity Worship

Do you remember the first time you became enamored with a celebrity? Do you remember who you admired and looked up to during different times in your life? For some of us, it's an athlete who peaks our interest and makes us opine to be like them. For others, it's an actor or actress. For still others, it's a writer or a politician or a wealth of other public figures that tickles our fancy and gains our adoration.

In the 1950s, the term 'parasocial interactions' described the relationships that individuals often feel toward celebrities and early television personalities (Massey, 2015). In other words, we watch celebrities and we enjoy them so much that we create an imaginary relationship with them. This imaginary relationship that we have with them influences our behaviors. We tend to act like them and follow them.

A 2006 study by Boon and Lomore investigated the degree that celebrity idols influenced young adults' perceptions of their identity and self-worth. It found that ninety percent of individuals felt feelings of attachment to a celebrity at some point in their development. Furthermore, seventy-five percent of individuals feel like they had strong attachments to more than one celebrity or national figure. There is most certainly a delusional component to these findings and one that reveals a very dangerous trend.

When we look up to celebrities, we feel close to them. This delusion creates a dynamic wherein we often want to *be* them. A study by Greene and Adams-Price (1990) confirmed that about thirty percent of us actually want to *be* the people we admire who have achieved celebrity status.

This phenomenon is the suicide of the self. It demonstrates an utter lack of self-confidence and a desire to abandon who we are in an attempt to be someone we aren't. If someone has a true sense of self, they do not need to find or create exterior representations to fulfill their aspirations of who they are. They are confident in their own skin and do not need exterior figures to model or create their sense of self.

However, with the rise of television in the 1950s, this concept of "parasocial interaction" has flooded and poisoned the American consciousness. Our perceived kinship with those who have been fortunate enough to be thrust upon the national stage, whether in sports or entertainment, influences the way we think and how we engage with others. It especially changes how we perceive ourselves. If we could only be like that celebrity we love, all our problems would melt away. This is the common thought process that is created by this parasocial interaction. There is no need to try to think of someone who exhibits this, albeit it should be an easy task. It is many of us, if we are being honest. There are not many people who have an intrinsic and well-developed sense of self who evade this phenomenon.

The advertisers know this. In the 1990s, the concept of reality shows was launched, starting with *The Real World*. Frankie, Ruthie, Jacinda, John, David, Kamaro and many more flooded our airwaves and created a new celebrity. The show required no writers or script. It was simply people just like us with cameras on them. Why did we watch? Because they were on TV and we related to them. They entered our homes and we bought into the illusion that we became part of their lives and that they became part of ours. This became the new "bread and circuses" for America as it brought celebrities and all the fantasies that come with celebrities even closer to home. It launched obsession in endless viewers' minds and hearts, and the marketing tactic worked extremely well. America was hooked. We paid less attention to who were leading us politically and more attention to what Snooki was doing.

Reality shows were like viruses that infected the diseased with a profound sense of vanity and nonsensical hysteria. The social media that rose in the late 1990s and early 2000s served to spread parasocial interaction like a pandemic. It, like TV, created pseudo-gods of others and further hampered the chances for us to develop our own senses of self. We became too preoccupied with looking at the qualities and traits of those who have achieved what our society has misleadingly deemed were the "holy grail" of being, that is, fame and fortune.

The recent development of "influencers" which occurred in the early 2010's illustrates this thesis. Celebrities continue to be our false idols. However, since celebrity-hood is exceedingly hard to achieve, we created our own celebrity. "Influencers" are people who gain widespread acclaim on a social media platform. This widespread acclaim, categorized by likes and views, mimics the celebrity-hood that so many of us get lost in admiring and striving to achieve. Social media enabled the creation of celebrities for the proletariat made by the proletariat. Anyone with an internet connection and a computer could be a celebrity.

This is where our society stands. We are a nation of celebrity worshipers. The select few who, let's face it, get lucky enough to be thrust into stardom are treated like the gods of ancient Rome. The great many of us are left sitting back and watching these individuals in awe and find ourselves emulating and creating fictitious relationships with these so-called "superior" people who, in reality, are just very fortunate versions of us.

German philosopher Friedrich Nietzsche (2005) commented on a similar type of so-called superior people in his philosophy. In his 1883 book *Thus Spoke Zarathustra*, he argues for the concept of the "*Übermensch*" as a goal for humanity. The *Übermensch*, which was translated by Walter Kaufman as "Overman," is a person who is posited to be superior to others and gives meaning to life on earth and who, for Nietzsche, replaces other-worldly concepts, focusing solely on this world. This Overman, Nietzsche argues, makes new values for humanity as it makes new meaning for humanity.

Modern-day celebrities, it becomes clear, fulfill many elements of Nietzsche's "*Übermensch*." In particular, the new meaning they tend to make for the masses and the erection of new, mostly self-serving values has much in common with Nietzsche's *Übermensch*. Modern-day celebrities, Nietzsche's Overman, are the very epitome of false idols that deceive the herd and do little more than pose as demigods delivering new and self-serving values for their own enrichment.

Enter advertising. Advertising is at the foundation of any capitalist system and implicitly utilizes the notion of the *Übermensch*. It is totally profit-driven, and therefore, it is totally amoral. Its sole mission and desire is to sell you whatever will make it profit. Therefore, advertising watches as our eyes gravitate toward the great and fortunate few who are given the breaks and chances necessary to ascend to celebrity status. Those in advertising see us watching and eagerly and greedily see this as their opening to manipulate and cajole us to spend our time and our money.

In the 1700s, Wedgewood, who was an English company who produced chinaware, used the endorsement of the King and Queen of England to exhibit the admirable and desirable qualities of having the product (NPR, 2012). This illustrates the ongoing attempts that advertisers made to manipulate individuals into believing their product was the best and in hoping to get them to trade their hard-earned dollars for the product.

In 1893, in England, Lillie Langtry became Pears Soap's poster girl and is the first recorded celebrity to endorse any commercial product. This concept of advertising spread very rapidly, and before long, advertisers realized that if they could tap into our celebrity lust and our lack of identities, they could make a fortune. And they did. (Morin, 2002)

In the 1990s, there was a basketball player who dominated the headlines and was considered by many to be the greatest basketball player who ever lived. Many still consider him to be the best today. Practically everyone who lived during the 1980s and 1990s can remember his influence on the game. Countless kids played ball pretending they were him and simulated scenarios in which they were emulating him in every way.

The advertisers, always lurking in the background, saw their opening. This player started appearing not only in basketball games but in an endless stream of commercials promoting an endless stream of products. One commercial that was particularly impactful, memorable, and, quite frankly, effective, featured his preferred method of hydrating himself. The commercial's refrain featured 'the great' player smiling and playing basketball for the Bulls and juxtaposed those images of him playing professionally with a group of regular people just like us in what looked like a local park. It played happy music in the background with a narrator singing this song,

"Sometimes I dream, that he is me / You've got to see that's how I dream to be / I dream I move / I dream I groove / Like Mike / Oh if I could be like Mike / Be like Mike, Be like Mike / Again I try / Just need to fly / For just one day I could be that way...." (PepsiCo, 1991).

The message is clear. If we want to be 'great' like the celebrity, we will buy the products because that will make us like him. When we become more like him, we will shed the identities we're trying to get away from and inherit his identity. This is the fallacy upon which the advertisers built a nation. This is why our identities are so diffuse and weak. Rather than try to build them up ourselves, we are too busy buying products and becoming like those who we believe we admire.

How do the advertising companies manipulate and coerce the masses into buying their products? The manipulation is wholly psychological. As researchers Choi and Rifon (2007) explain, obsession with celebrities characterizes the American identity today. This is used by the advertising companies to seize the attention of the consumer – us. They utilize very specific qualities of the endorsements they pick to target the minds and hearts of the population they are looking to sell the product or products. Research has shown since at least 1991, in a study by Ohanian and continued by Choi and Rifon, that there are specifically targeted attributes that celebrity endorsers must have for advertising companies to utilize them for the products. What are these impressionable qualities? Perceived attractiveness tops the list. I don't think that anyone can argue the veracity of this. Our advertisements are littered with people who meet today's arbitrary, societally created, and very narrow standards of beauty.

This cultural standard of beauty being something that we need to emulate has its origins in ancient Greece. There, aesthetic beauty determined a great deal of your status and your well-being in the social circles of the society. Being a good-looking man by Greek standards bought you status and privilege of all kinds. Boys who had any leisure time often spent that time at the gym, and that time at the gym usually paid dividends in Greek society. For women, beauty had different ramifications and was often a mixed bag. Hesiod, who was a major poet between 750-650 BC, coined the term 'kakon' or woman, which meant 'beautiful – evil thing.' Furthermore, there were routine beauty contests, called kallestia. We must never forget Homer's creation of Helen of Troy, or, "the face that launched a thousand ships" (Marlowe, 1969, p.93). Her beauty was so enigmatic and overwhelming that it spawned one of the most important wars in Greek history. This is where we see the utilization of beauty to manipulate and cajole people into acting in ways that they wouldn't normally act. (BBC News, 2015).

The advertisers of any capitalist society understand the lessons of ancient Greece. They utilized this cultural yearning to be aesthetically pleasing that the Greeks created. This became the first pillar of how they could change the way we thought about a product or create a need for what they wanted. The thought process sounds like this: if beautiful people are doing it, you should do it too. You want to be beautiful like these people, don't you?

This endless desire for beauty makes you want to spend your money. However, how can you be sure the product is good just because the person is beautiful? This is where the concept of trustworthiness enters into the advertising picture. The second major pillar of advertising manipulation involves trustworthiness. The people who use a company's products not only have to be beautiful, but they have to make us believe that the products will be good for us. Since we identify with them, this is not a hard or far-fetched task. This becomes a careful balancing act for advertising. If any celebrity endorses too many products, they can be seen as untrustworthy. Therefore the concept of trustworthiness is a very careful creation on the side of advertisers as they shape and mold the celebrity to appeal to our faith in them. The thought process looks something like this. "I feel like I know this singer because I get the lyrics, and I get them, and I think they get me. Therefore, whatever they buy, I trust because they know what it's like." It is this personal relationship and the carefully cultivated image of trustworthiness that enables us to open our wallets or purses and contribute to the celebrity's cause.

Another major tool of advertising manipulation is the concept of expertise. Pick your favorite celebrity. Every one of them has an area in which they should have agency for expertise. Any athlete is going to be able to tell you what footwear, jersey, training materials, or athletic equipment to buy in an uncontested way. Who would know better than a great home run hitter as to what baseball bat you should purchase? Similarly, who could possibly have a better handle on beautiful makeup or what dress you should wear then the latest fashion model or great actress who is known for her beauty? These arguments of authority are another major factor in how advertisers cajole and influence our minds with the endless onslaught of images and sounds that we hear every day. They entice us the way they enticed the fictional Chris. We learn to buy whatever thing we 'need' to buy to continue to fit in or belong in any way to a society that is all focused on belonging and totally unfocused on what we actually need.

If we buy the products, we can relate and be ever closer to our false idols: the celebrities. If we continue to create this kinship with our celebrities, we can shed our own uncreated and unfulfilled identities and aspire to attain theirs. This cycle leaves us endlessly unfulfilled and painfully unsatisfied. It is a recipe for psychological disaster. Socrates, who belongs to the ancient Greek club I mentioned before, told us that we have to, "Know thyself" (Ekanem, p. 69). The existentialists told us that we have to create our own identity in order to create our own world that is meaningful to us. These and many other psychologists, philosophers, and great minds told us that the first step in creating a better life and world for ourselves is to understand who we are and what we want out of it. In fact, the very term 'psychology' comes from Latin and Greek origins that mean, 'the study of the mind' or 'the study of the soul' (Merriam-Webster Dictionary, 2024). The very term implicitly states that navigating the mind is a voyage of the self.

Our society prefers to substitute this search for the self with the search for the desire to be someone else. Between 4,000 and 10,000 times each day, every day, the engine described above may flood our minds and rend our consciousness. 'If we only dressed like her, our lives would be easy. If we just had a body like him, our woes would end. If we don't act this way, we won't be accepted in the group or the club that we want to be around.' The endless onslaught of images and concepts confuses us as to who we are and steers us far off the path of finding ourselves. They are the true false idols that we are asked to worship at the altar of economics and greed. And every day that they get stronger, we get weaker. Our identities diminish little by little and ebb away as we slowly wade into the cold waters of conformity and accept our fates. We entertain ourselves with the "bread and circuses" that we are given and never seek communion with or get in touch with ourselves. Because somewhere along the line we gained the notion that being alienated is the worst of all possible worlds. We seek comfort in whatever societally created concepts we find attractive and think we want to emulate and never for a moment pay attention to our true selves. What is more tragic than that? We've become nations of sycophants pining to be whatever we aren't and running from being whatever we are.

American political scientist Francis Fukuyama (2006) alludes to a similar cycle of desire in his book, *The End of History and the Last Man*. He notes, "Men are made unhappy not because they fail to gratify some fixed set of desires, but by the gap that continually arises between new wants and their fulfillment" (Fukuyama, 2006). The gap that continually arises between our wants and our fulfillment is a seemingly endless parade of false idols that we create for ourselves and is funneled and fed to us for our constant consumption.

This trend is only getting worse. Why is it getting worse? Because it is so profitable and because the formula works. As noted, this formula was always profitable and dates back prior to the inception of mass media. However, each new advent of technology brings with it a new way for advertisers to waive the allure of celebrity before our faces (Drake et al., 2010). Going to public events such as plays and musicals was great, but advertisers saw that radio could reach a lot more people at one time. Radio worked well, but advertisers saw that television could include the preeminent sense of sight and that we had an easier time remembering what we saw and what we heard. Television is extremely effective, but the Internet was infinitely more versatile and accessible to the needs of the common person. The Internet was amazing, but social media, as a subcategory of the Internet, was where everybody connected and delivering messages through social media has become amongst the supreme ways to manipulate and deliver these messages to the masses.

This concept of celebrity worship and self-neglect is becoming a worldwide phenomenon. Researchers Francis and Yazdinafard (2013) have noted that the influence of celebrities and their impact on our lives exists in Europe, the United States, and the Far East, among other places. For instance, they write, "Meanwhile, in India, celebrities are being worshipped like "idols" to the masses, and would follow them and even wait for them in droves at events such as a filming of a movie" (Francis and Yazdinafard, 2013, p. 36). In Far East nations, South Korea especially, celebrities are being culturally hybridized with the American celebrity culture after the Korean wave of music and movies. The pop band Seo Taiji and Boys and the film Sopyonje received critical acclaim in their respective field for their depiction about Korean culture and daily life (Shin, 2011). It is conceivable that every industrialized nation will be and perhaps already is following this format of the diversion and celebrity worship that does nothing but distract us from not only ourselves, but, I would argue, what truly matters.

The use of celebrity has worked so well in achieving capitalistic goals that it was aimed to achieve that many different formulas have been used to entice prospective purchasers to emulate the celebrity with whom they have an imagined relationship. As long as the endorser is well-liked by the public, it has been found that it does not even matter if the endorser and the product are a good match (Francis and Yazdinafard, 2013). In other words, we will buy whatever the person we look up to tells us to buy. This is, perhaps, *the* definition of a weak ego. When we are children, and we have very little conception of self, we tend to emulate whatever our favorite parent does. Can you remember using some nebulous tool to try to shave our faces just like Dad used to do years before we even had facial hair? On the female side, I would project that women may have tried to emulate their moms putting on makeup doing their hair a certain way. We emulate what we look up to instinctually. But at some point, we should feel strong enough in our sense of self to shed the desire to be like anyone else but ourselves. The concept of celebrity suppresses this desire and keeps us constantly and aimlessly searching to be like whoever it is we think we want to emulate. The advertisers have understood the psychology all too well. So when our favorite movie star tells us to buy something that they are absolutely unqualified to tell us to buy, we revert to that little boy or girl within us who wants to be like mom, dad, or whoever else we came to admire.

The only time this phenomenon backfires is when the celebrity overshadows the brand. This has actually been called the 'vampire effect,' and it is well documented in the literature (Francis and Yazdinafard, 2013). Celebrities have come to be in over 20% of our ads. The only rule that the advertising world seems to abide by is that the celebrity cannot overshadow the brand. Because if the celebrity does, they become, in some ways, a liability in selling the brand. Therefore, the second your favorite celebrity is more remembered than the product the celebrity is trying to sell, they are pulled. In other words, nothing is allowed to get more attention than the almighty product.

All of this manipulation that is being done every moment of every day in the United States and across the world relies on our tacit agreement and willingness to be manipulated. As noted, in the 1950s, researchers coined the term 'parasocial interaction.' It was used to describe the phenomenon of the imaginary relationships that consumers felt for the early television performers. Television was invented in 1946. As soon as society could not only hear but also see their favorite performers, everything changed. This concept of parasocial interaction created a new psychological dynamic that had never been seen in such a widespread way in all of history. The research suggested that the feelings we create for our celebrities can play a major role in our conception of ourselves and our perception of the world around us (Massey, 2015).

Who among us can say this is not true? I describe the relationship with our parents above and how we tend to emulate the parent or caretaker with whom we are most enamored growing up. They become our model for existence, and as any therapist, including this one, will tell you, it is this model that changes our behavior and our conception of the world from childhood onward. In fact, we often spend much of our time analyzing and understanding our patient's past relationship with her parents. This has been as true since the creation of psychotherapy in the 1890s by Sigmund Freud as it is now. There is no denying the impact of our parents or caretakers being our first role models for us and, especially in those crucial developmental years that so many psychologists and especially those in the psychoanalytic realm, hold up as the most crucial time of our development.

However, what always seemed tragic is that we tend to stop analyzing the effect of role models in childhood. Our development covers our lifespan. Our connections cannot be marginalized or narrowed to just those we encountered and bonded with during a very early period in our developments. We find meaning in many connections and all of those connections come to shape and forge who we are and, what we believe, and what creates purpose and meaning for us.

This is where the concept of parasocial interaction becomes so important. Researcher Susan Boon of Calgary University conducted a survey in 2006 in which she found that ninety percent of us felt that we had a strong relationship with a celebrity at some point in our lives. Furthermore, she found that seventy-five percent of us report we have "strong attachments" to more than one celebrity. A different study by Green and Adams-Price (1990) found that thirty percent of us actually wanted to be the celebrity we admire.

This evidence begins to illustrate a bigger picture. Psychological development does not stop at 8 or 10 or 12 or 15, or 20 years old. It seems clear that it never stops. As discussed, our parents or caretakers serve as our role models who we emulate early. Celebrities fill the unnecessary void from the moment we stop cleaving to our caretakers' image. They play an immensely important role in our sense of self, and the role that they come to play has a heavy influence on who we become and especially on who we want to become. They ensure that we never have to deal with the muddy and difficult process of getting to know ourselves because we are always reaching and seeking to know them and be them.

This is where advertisers step in like parasites. They serve an essentially parasitic function by praying on our weak senses of self. They see the bigger picture in our disillusionment and fill the void of our existences through the use of the allure of the celebrity to show us who we think we want to be.

The root problem, then, is our sense of self. Our identity is very impacted by this concept of parasocial interaction and it impacts a great deal of our society. If we are all running around trying to be like someone else, we are never paying attention to anything that matters. Look at any celebrity's social media account if evidence is needed of this thesis. On any social media site, you will find a carefully constructed shadow of the celebrity image. I say shadow because it is an image and an image alone, just as their existences are all carefully constructed capitalistic images designed to create profit and emulation and adoration. There was a day when this was a much more arduous process, and people had to send letters or find the physical addresses of where a celebrity gets their mail. Now, it is as easy as a few keystrokes and clicks to bond with that person who really, "gets you" even though you've never spoken a single word to them.

Social media has made this disconnection from self greater than it's ever been in our existences. Now, we can simulate the fantasy role of a celebrity by using our social media accounts. Even the terminology of social media encourages and overtly elicits the concept of celebrity. The vast majority of social media websites use the term "followers." Some pertinent synonyms are a fan, worshiper, admirer, groupie, devotee, acolyte, and you get the point. What are the terms that are used for people who adore celebrities? They are exactly the same. This helps promote the unconscious delusion of being a celebrity. Social media has created a world in which everyone can create the illusion that they are a celebrity and that they are like their favorite celebrity.

However, this is only an illusion. It is a very, very dangerous illusion. Parasocial interaction creates a mental setting of dissociation. It creates a world wherein you get further from who you are and indulge in a fantasy world that indulges dreams, illusions, and mirages of what you imagine would be perfect places.

It also must be emphasized just like the social media profiles we view, all celebrities themselves are largely social constructions. The image that is created is solely a social creation. It is erected on ideals and absolutes and marketing principles and not feelings and warmth and humanity. While, of course, they are real people, they are created in the image of something eternal, infallible, and almost beyond human. This is a large part of what attracts us to them. It is the concept of perfection for some and adoration for others. All celebrity worship fills some deep-seated psychological yearning. However, rather than seek to understand why we have that psychological need, we repress that impulse and hurl ourselves into the desire to satiate a need that, quite frankly, will never be satiated by celebrity.

As a therapist, I often inquire as to my client's role model. I like to understand who they look up to or admire and who they see as heroes. I often have people say all kinds of names, from singers to athletes to politicians. As I explore their thoughts, it becomes clear that many cannot have very healthy relationships with celebrities. In other words, we can't just admire someone else without it rising to parasocial interaction. This can remain good and healthy and often serves as a way to cultivate the concept of purpose. However, more often than not, I see this pathology rooted in a much darker origin. I see the admiration for a celebrity as a coping mechanism to escape their own pathology. I see alternate worlds created by new celebrities who serve to insulate the pain of a broken identity. It is this broken identity that I find will never heal if it is being propped up by an illusion. It is only by pulling the illusion out of their psyches and holding them up for them to see for change to occur. Recognizing that celebrity worship is not going to make you who you want to be is often the beginning of change.

A 2009 study by Gayle Stever in the *Journal of Media Psychology* gives some insight into celebrity worship and some of the psychological pitfalls of parasocial interaction. She discusses the differentiation between fans suffering from pathologies and fans who are healthy. She notes that a small amount of extremely obsessive fans actually have the potential to harm themselves or the celebrities with whom they have the parasocial relationship (Stever, 2009). This study demonstrates the severe and occasionally dark psychological effect that these parasocial relationships can have on our psyches.

Without knowing ourselves, we cannot progress in almost any definition of the term progress. Without progressing, we stay static, still, disconnected. It is that disconnection that is being actively cultivated by not only the capitalist advertisers, but by the society at large. As long as we are running around groping in the dark to find a celebrity who we think will "make us whole" or who "really understands us," we will remain in the dark.

Celebrity worship keeps us in this dark world wherein we cannot know ourselves because we are trying to be something else. Celebrity worship is, then, one of the "bread and circuses" that distract us from ourselves and from any purpose or meaning that we find in this existence. It is, unlike many of our challenges in life, not something that has to exist in any way. We created this concept. It came out of our own pain and the psychological issues that created that pain. Celebrity worship diverts us from our inadequacies and serves as one great bandage to distract us from our self. In addition to distracting us from ourselves, it serves to be the fuel that runs the engine of greed that is conceived to "propel" our society forward while at the same time poisoning it to the prospect of progress.

Chapter 3

Economic Culture

Celebrity culture and celebrity worship are one facet of the greater concept of economic culture. Economic culture is pervasive and dominating and, in many ways, is the driving force behind all false idols. The concept of economic culture is enormous in scope and intrinsically impacts every breath we take in whatever continent we live. That is because economics is essentially the study of the distribution of the total amount of resources that any society has. We are not born self-sufficient. Human beings need many material goods at any given time in our lives. Therefore, the study of how the goods and services that we need are distributed amongst human beings is intrinsically important to every beating heart. In other words, we could not exist without economics. It is unavoidable and it has existed as long as human beings have existed.

The industrialized Western world has, in widely varying degrees, adopted some form of capitalism as a model or at least a part of their economic theory. The United States, for instance, has wrapped both arms around this concept of capitalism and held very tightly. Capitalism, then, forms the keystone of economic culture that pervades the United States and, to a lesser degree, many other Western European countries. (Boettke and Heilbroner, 2023)

In 1776, *An Inquiry into the Nature and Causes of The Wealth of Nations* was published by Adam Smith. This book created the foundational concepts of capitalism. Without going too deeply into his many assertions and precepts, it is based on the concept of a free and open market. A free and open market necessitates that business owners compete with each other to produce a product that the public will purchase. The creation of wealth, then, is the greatest goal of the capitalist economic system. The creation of wealth is the goal of the economic culture that pervades many countries, such as the United States. This is despite the fact that Christianity is one of the dominant religions there, and, Christianity abhors the accumulation of wealth. The clash between these two cultural concepts has always provided a certain overwhelming hypocrisy. In many ways, it is truly the clash of two idols to be worshiped.

It is undeniable, however, that the basis of capitalism is competition. Competition breeds anger, envy, and disdain of every kind (also values that contradict Christian theology and philosophy). From Adam Smith's point of view, this competition creates widely available products expediently, creates wealth, and widespread incentives. There is no denying that this is true. It forces anyone creating a product to find the cheapest way to create that product so that they could sell the most and make the most money. The competition that fuels this quest for the most money creates a wide variety of byproducts that produce an enormous gross domestic product and, therefore, production of capital. The competition that underlies all of these processes creates a distance or alienation between the people living under such a system.

What does this mean? It means that if we spend our lives trying to get what someone else has for ourselves, we lose sight of anything else but that sense of competition. Competition forges our worldview toward gaining wealth and beating each other out with all of the same zeal that a blacksmith forges metal into whatever creation he wants. If you are always trying to get a car like your neighbor has, a house like a neighbor has, a husband, a wife, a bigger yard, pool, or any other material desire that you have a value for, what else do you see in life? Competition shifts our values and forces us to pursue things about which we often don't care. Much of our quests tend to be in search of this material existence that is everlastingly unfulfilling. In many ways, competition creates the proverbial carrot that serves as the fuel for any capitalist system.

This fuel creates the culture. This culture consumes much of our thought, lives, and heartbeats on this earth. Let me operationalize this concept using an example to which most of us can relate.

Remember Chris and Joelle? Let's say Joelle applies for and gains a new job. Her motive for getting the job is to gain more income for her family, and especially for Dominic's college fund. The job is difficult, and she has to gain new skills to work at it. She automatically compares herself to all of her coworkers with similar titles and seeks to find ways that she can outperform them or provide something unique to her employer. She talks to and befriends many of her coworkers but both her coworkers and her have the implicit burden of having to compete with each other for the greatest output so that they can create the most wealth for the company. By creating the most wealth for the company, they have the opportunity to create the most wealth for themselves by virtue of getting rewarded for creating the most wealth. The thin veneer of humanity that she expresses for her coworkers and that her coworkers express for the supervisor is skin deep since it is self-interest that is really important to each of them. At the end of every day, Joelle simply wants to go back to her family with the most amount of wealth that she can attain to do what she perceives as bettering her family's life.

The tiers of competition in this vignette are many. The capitalist system and macroeconomic concept hovers in the background. In other words, all of Joelle's existence at the agency that she works for is based on that agency. Therefore, the macro competition that her agency is doing with the other agencies that it competes with is the background upon which all other competition is fostered. The micro competition of Joelle's title in employment with the other individuals who have the same title and employment is what Joelle sees every day because that is all that matters to her. She simply wants to be a valued employee who can gain the most amount of income for her family.

Joelle spends about one third of her existence at this agency every day. Another third of her existence is spent in sleep. Finally, the other one-third of her life is spent with what she actually values, which is her family with Dominic and Chris.

Therefore, the false idol that Joelle chases is finances. Thirty percent of her life is spent wrapped up in competing in a game she never wanted to play to get the money that she feels compelled to get due to the economic culture around her.

Joelle always wanted to be a painter. She always wanted to learn the salsa and has a great deal of interest in dancing lessons of any kind. She would love nothing more than to spend every moment looking into her baby's eyes and seeing a glimpse of heaven when she looks into them. These, and her husband, her parents, and her collection of books are what she loves most in the world. These are what she values. However, she is stuck chasing a distraction because that is what our economic culture has stated she has to do.

Economic culture is the mores, belief systems, and philosophies that our economic system imprints onto all of the minds of those who live in it. Joelle's plight is many of our plights, and it is indicative of the impact of economic culture. We have ceased being who we want to be and instead are competing with each other to be something that we were made to believe we want to be. It is no different than celebrity culture and celebrity worship in that it is appealing to our eyes and our hopes and creates models for self-concepts in a direction that is very often completely opposite of the direction that we want to go. Our economic culture is hinged on the concept that accumulating personal wealth is the meaning of life. Our general spiritual consciousness is hinged on the concept that collecting pieces of paper with the faces of dead presidents on them was never intended to be our purpose and mission in life. This tension is strong and severe and overtakes us from a very young age. We are inundated with the concept that the greatest virtue is to chase wealth. Ironically, many of the heroes who we hold up in our culture behaved in exactly the opposite way. Mahatma Gandhi, Jesus Christ, George Orwell, Leo Tolstoy, and Mother Teresa are just a few of the people who are held in high esteem while simultaneously embracing a life of material scarcity. Our economic system preaches the opposite of their messages. It tells us to worship wealth, and that poverty is somehow associated with all things negative. It seems a contradiction to love or admire figures like these in an economic culture that heavily influences us to hold the utterly opposite set of values they had. As a result, the millions of individuals who are in poverty in the United States live with an immense stigma. I won't cite the actual statistics because the federal government's "poverty line" is so low that it is blatantly absurd. It does not come close to capturing the plight of the destitute in this country.

The stigma that those suffering from poverty suffer is another part of the economic culture of coercion that occurs endlessly in our lives. Mark Rank, social welfare professor at the Brown School of Washington University in St. Louis states that, "Within the United States, we tend to view poverty as an issue of 'them' rather than 'us,'" and he goes on to state, "those in poverty are seen as strangers to mainstream America, people of color, falling outside of acceptable behavior, and as such, to be scored and stigmatized" (Schoenherr, 2021).

It is stigmatization, then, rather than acceptance and compassion that we as a society view and treat those in poverty, despite the admiration we have for the select few individuals who came from poverty. This is a direct result of economic culture. It creates the false idol of wealth and holds it very high in millions of people like Joelle, who are stuck reaching for something that consumes most of their lives but means very little. This hegemony, or dominance of one belief system over another, serves as an everlasting distraction from how we want to live our lives due to a cultural force that tells us how we must live our lives.

Now that the divisiveness that economic culture creates is clear, let's examine some of the precepts of this culture of division.

Our economic culture tells us that, as Michael Douglas's character in *Wall Street* (1987) states, "greed is good." It tells us that the goal of life involves accumulating the most wealth or material for yourself. This concept leaves us forever unsatisfied and looking up to this all too real one percent of the population who owns almost all of the wealth. This mindset makes false idols out of rich people. These false idols create a sort of wealth worship that dominates our society. Economic culture is responsible for the way we perceive the accumulation of goods and why we perceive it that way. It goes further by culturally dividing the populace into gradations of individuals who have and have less.

Over time, this concept runs amok. The value of one's bank account and total assets is gradually seen by the culture as the value of one's worth. Over time, the two concepts of work become confused. People with wealth culturally ascend to a greater status in society and are seen to 'have' greater worth than those who do not have wealth. This ascension in the consciousness of the culture is exhibited by how much those who have wealth are being seen, how much they are lauded, how many times we hear their names mentioned in an adoring or awe-inspiring way for their economic pursuits.

The concept of greed and the accumulation of wealth are dehumanizing, then, by definition. It asks us to value something other than basic human worth. This serves as an everlasting imposing hegemonic distraction to how we conceive of and entertain the idea of self-worth. The thought process becomes, "if I do not have money or goods, I am not as good as others." It is with this mindset that we collectively send our children off into a world that will only reinforce this concept over and over again. The most absurd aspect of this concept is how efficient this false idol is. According to the Federal Reserve (2021), the top one percent of income earners in the United States owned 32.3% of the country's wealth. The bottom fifty percent of the country's population held 2.6% of the country's wealth. Therefore, due in great part to this concept of economic culture and the misleading capitalistic doctrine that "greed is good," 99% of the population seeks to idolize and envy the identity of the 1%. This is another form of self-suicide at the behest of a culturally created myth. As long as these distracting "bread and circuses" are formed in the ideologies of chasing wealth, the power structure created by them will continue. It is only by recognizing the absurdity of these concepts that we can begin to shed them and live by what we truly value or not by what we are told to value by our economic mores and cultural beliefs.

This devotion to greed and the belief that it is part of the purpose of our existence is how another major part of our economic system oppresses us. This is by exploitation. It is our readiness to believe that if we just work hard enough we can have all that that one percent has that enables us to be exploited on the widespread and massive levels that we are.

Let's go back to Joelle. She took that new job believing it would solve all of the economic woes that it would give her the quality of life that she believed she needed. However, the supervisor at her new job was not nearly as gracious or kind as the supervisor in her old job. She was told she was unable to earn what she thought she would earn when she took the job due to shifts in management. She was told she had to take on significantly more work than she did at her old job which caused her an immense amount more stress. She had to deal with misogyny and other forms of mistreatment due to her work culture. Finally, she signed up for a forty-hour work week and ended up working sixty hours most weeks due to the massive amount of work she had to get done with her new workload.

Joelle protested, and protested often. She approached her supervisor, she approached her supervisor's supervisor, and even went to corporate regarding her complaints. However, at every turn, she was told that they could not help her. There was no union and she had no one else to turn to for help. So she decided to just put her head down and continue to work with the thought of providing for her son, Dominic.

This is exploitation. It, along with greed and competition, form the three heads of capitalistic economic culture. This three-headed monster wreaks havoc on our psyches, health, and sense of well-being. Cerberus was the mythological figure in ancient Greece that was depicted as a three-headed and very vicious dog that guarded the gates of Hades to ensure that no one could escape. Economic culture, represented by its version of Cerberus, a three-headed monster of greed, competition, and exploitation, serves as the guard that ensures that we cannot escape the mental oppression of our existence. It is only by recognizing the false idol that is being presented before us that we can consciously learn to change the way we view it and live our lives the way we want to live them.

Chapter 4

Sports

Sports are transcendent. No matter what color or creed, no matter what gender or sexuality, religion or culture, sports tend to appeal to individuals of all shapes and sizes. Sports both unite and divide. However, the division is often overlooked in light of the fact that sports provide community, a common bond, and a sense of unity amongst its fans. How many of us identify ourselves as a fan of a certain team? How many of us look at the fellow fans of our team as a sort of non-sanguine brother or sister? Sports are a source of pleasure, a source of joy, and a source for us to feel connected in a way that we fail to feel connected throughout our very lives.

Every sport is composed of a large number of athletes who have never met us and, by and large, have no interest in meeting us. Some of the obvious motives for playing the sport they play are to make money, enjoy the sport that they grew up and excelled at playing, and, if they are so inclined and physically gifted, to be a legendary athlete that children and adults alike look up to and emulate. They have a very short playing career in most cases and typically use their moments in the limelight to acquire the maximum amount of both prestige and compensation so that they can live off of their earnings after their short career is done.

We, as fans, pay those earnings. Buying memorabilia in the form of jerseys, signed articles, and tickets are just a few of the ways we contribute to their livelihood financially. Many of us dedicate our time and resources to learning nebulous stats and keeping up with everything that our favorite player or team is doing. In many cases, we get obsessed. As I write this, for instance, there is a movie that illustrates a group of women who are obsessed with a specific player on a specific team. The entire plot of the movie is based around their sports fanaticism.

The psychological underpinnings of why we love sports seem obvious. Whether it is the community they create, the common bonds they cultivate, or the excitement and suspense that they provide, they fill a void in each fan's psyche. Many of us have met someone who stakes their entire identity on being the most devoted fan. This is the person who paints their face in the team colors, owns rare and very difficult-to-get artifacts and memorabilia of their favorite players and team, and prides themselves on knowing every statistic for both the team and the individuals they love on the team. Sports play a major role in many cultures, and American culture is certainly no exception to this rule. The Super Bowl XLIX, for instance, had an incredible one hundred million viewers in the United States alone (Pallota, 2015). European soccer, Indian and Australian cricket, Canadian hockey, and so many other sports create wellsprings of entertainment, joy, community, and identity for the billions of fans who watch them.

Juvenal himself used to watch sports in ancient Rome, and it was very likely one of the "bread and circuses" he was referring to in his discourse. He discussed how gladiators often enjoyed the attention of Roman women. The concept of the gladiator was born from Etruscan funerals. The gladiator who died was meant to be an offering for the dead person to have in the afterlife as an attendant. It dates back to at least two hundred and sixty-four B.C. (Editors of Encyclopedia Britannica, 2023) The concept of a gladiator can undoubtedly be interpreted as another 'bread and circus' to distract and entertain the Roman people so that they do not revolt. As further proof of this, the Roman government created these bouts to the death for free. They were merely a way to get the masses to think about and get excited about anything but their plight. If they did not think about the plight, then they would not revolt. Events in the Coliseum, the Circus Maximus, the theaters, the plays, and so on were all ways for the Roman government to distract the people. This was the method of oppression created by the Roman government, and it continues to be the method of oppression some two thousand five hundred years later in the Western world. (Wabash College, 2023).

In this way, modern-day sports are the ancient Roman sports of the Coliseum. They have a way of uniting, a way of creating camaraderie, and they have immense entertainment value. However, if we are looking at the situation from afar, it seems clear that they are also one enormous distraction to make sure that the masses, and in particular those who don't have material wealth, are kept complacent.

How many people could accurately answer the question of what quarterback won the most Super Bowls of all time? However, if you asked the same people what president created the most opportunities for individuals in poverty, what kind of answer would be given? We know more about star athletes than we do about James Madison, James Monroe, James Buchanan, or James Garfield combined. We can have more intelligent, knowledgeable, and detailed conversations about who is the greatest ice hockey player of all time than we can about who is the babysitter who watches our very children.

Sports are beautiful. They are amongst the greatest inventions of human beings and many of us truly enjoy engaging in and watching them. However, there is something in us that allows them to become more like a religion then a respite. Athletes are proficient at kicking and catching, at throwing and hurling.

They have superior physical strength and their lung capacity and ability to engage in running and other activities is astounding and admirable and impressive in every way imaginable.

However, this does not make them gods. They are not above anyone else and the only reason that they have anything that they have is because we give it to them. The more time that we spend indulging their vanity and making them the super-humans they have become in the public eye, the less we see and tend to be cognizant of those who are lusting for personal power.

According to a nationwide survey done in February 2022, the average American dedicates four hours to sports watching every week. Over one-fifth or 23% of Americans, watch more than five hours per week. In addition, the average American watches 1.3 hours of sports highlights per week. Given the tremendous weight of responsibility that our culture places on earning money, this is a significant amount of time. There is a heavy gender bias here wherein males watch sports more than twice as much, averaging 5.8 hours per week. Females watch about 2.6 hours of sports each week. Interestingly, males overwhelmingly prefer to watch sports alone, and it is that solitude that may help cultivate their parasocial relationships with the players and coaches. (Ivanovska, 2023).

These statistics reveal that sports-watching is pervasive among the American populace. Whether it is football or hockey, baseball or basketball, we are hooked. It is, for many of us, an addiction. That addiction engages us for a wide variety of psychological reasons.

This addiction mimics the celebrity addiction noted in the aforementioned chapter. The modern-day gladiators that entertain us by sacrificing, in many cases, both their bodies and brains simply appeal to a different demographic, at least in the United States. The same concept of the herd instinct prevails and pervades the minds of men and women across the nation. The athletes are elevated to superior status and emulated, and the fact that some of them make more in a single game than many of us do in our entire lives is gleefully ignored and forgotten for the sake of the emotional rush that we get from watching them for what in most cases is less than three hours at a sitting.

However, it is our right to spend our leisure time in anyway we please within the realm of legality and decency toward each other, right? This is probably a fair statement, and most Americans and human beings would agree.

It doesn't, however, take into consideration the economic concept of opportunity cost. According to Adam Carpenter of the U.S. News & World Report (2022), opportunity cost is, "a benefit that an individual or business forgoes because they made one decision instead of another" (para. 1). In other words, it is what was forfeited by our making one choice over the other choice.

This concept is a crucial economic concept. Each choice that we make with our capital limits other choices that we could've made to gain other things that we may have wanted.

Why do I bring up this concept of opportunity cost? Due to the roughly 302 hours per year that every male spends watching sports and adoring the modern-day gladiators of our time, he could've been doing something else. For the cost of watching sports for around thirteen full days of this year, he could've been engaged in charity work or helping a friend or making the world in our society the smallest bit of a better place. However, this distraction ensures that he will not do that. The "bread and circuses" that he spends his time watching guarantee that his mind is enraptured with statistics and theatrics rather than those aspects of his existence that benefit him more directly as well as those around him.

Most of all, however, the false idols that sports have become in our culture take us away from our civic duty. In the same survey I previously referenced, 65% of the American populace would rather watch sports than news. To put that in perspective, almost seven out of ten people would rather lose themselves in a game that is ultimately meaningless to their lives rather than watch what is going on around them so they can be better informed on how to create a better life for themselves and their families. They would rather know how many goals a star hockey player scored than know the dollars the representative they voted for allocated to their district to help them and their families get through the rough economic year that they are experiencing. As Shakespeare said, "there's the rub" (3.1 65). Watching sports, as discussed, is wonderful and creates immense satisfaction in the watcher and most importantly, it unites us in feeling connected to our fellow human being. However, they also serve as another red herring that keeps us from making our lives and the lives of those around us better in every way.

The advertisers see this. They see the immense amount of excitement and interest that both men and women have for all kinds of sports. And it is with the same seething greed and opportunistic desire that they swoop in and begin feeding off of the distracted minds of the masses.

According to the Washington Journal (Bruell, 2020), during Super Bowl LV, on February 7, 2021, CBS charged $5.5 million per commercial for the Super Bowl. Think about that for a minute. Most of us will not see one-fifth of $5.5 million in our lifetimes, no matter how hard we work. However, advertising is willing to spend those incredible amounts of money for a mere thirty seconds so that they can gain your attention and sell their products. It is this kind of economic absurdity that we have learned to worship rather than learn to revolt against it.

Not only do we not revolt against it, we champion it. How many of us congregate around the water coolers in our offices and talk about how funny this commercial was or that commercial was or, who this commercial had in it and how we love that person?

By definition, every NFL game is one hour in length. There are obviously starts and stops of the clock based on incomplete passes, halftime, possession changes, penalties, and a wide range of other issues that occur. Therefore, it is reasonable to say that an NFL game should take something like an hour and forty-five minutes or so in its entirety if it was being played all at the same time. However, advertisers and other parasitic entities that are feeding off of our interests make the average game into a three hour affair. The Super Bowl is sometimes lengthened to an incredible four hours. Over 25% of any NFL game is commercials and while those commercials do not command the price tag and interest of the ones in the Super Bowl, every game is purely a financial enterprise. That financial enterprise is geared at gaining your attention and creating false idols for you to become enamored with or want to emulate. The false idols who we have these parasocial relationships with sacrifice themselves in hopes of generating money for the advertisers and, ultimately, themselves. It can be seen as a sick, sad, and twisted system that creates and fosters psychological dependence, emotional and mental harm, and financial harm to many of us who spend our time engaging with it. This is not to mention the fact that sports advertising actively serves as a red herring that distracts us from our civic duties. It especially does so at a time when civic participation is needed more than ever to create a habitable society or commonwealth that adequately serves all.

It is not sports. It is the intentional and disproportionate focus that we are actively cultivated to have for them that serves to pull us away from the aspects of life that require constant attention.

Let's examine sports advertising to get a broader concept of the depth and breadth of this issue. Researcher Manoli (2017) stated that in 2015, the advertising industry in sports was amongst the fastest-growing revenue streams. He noted that forty-five billion dollars were spent in the United States alone on advertising in sports in 2015. Forty-five billion dollars. To put this in context, the United States budget contained around twenty-nine billion dollars for school lunches, and that was seven years after this study, in 2022 (Statista, 2022).

The global sports industry itself costs in the neighborhood of one hundred forty-five billion dollars according to Manoli (2017). This figure accounts for around 3% of the entire global economy. In other words, about 3% of every exchange in every nation on the face of the earth is an exchange that promotes sports. That number is not shrinking as people find more and more sanctuary in sports. This is especially true as sports get increasingly marketed in a way that demands more and more of our attention and interest and zeal.

As evidence of this, one only has to look at the evolving number of the forty-five billion dollars that was accredited to the sports in the United States in 2015. This figure grew to be an enormous $71.06 billion in 2018. That is a 37% jump. And it just gets bigger. The same source, Statista.com, states that it is forecasted to be $83.1 billion by 2023. The marketing is working and people are watching and less and less interest is getting paid to the other parts of our existence that matter. (Manoli 2017).

Considering these figures, the connection between the economy and sports has clearly become extreme and shows no signs of stopping. According to ESPN, United States sports betting was a $10.9 billion industry in 2023 (Greenberg, 2024). Gambling is obviously very popular and there is a neurochemical basis for this false idol to be erected in the lives of many sports fans. Gambling and the increased impulsivity that accompanies it are linked to dopamine and dopamine is a prime motivator of gambling behavior, according to researchers Anselme and Robinson of *Frontiers of Behavioral Neuroscience* (2013). Gambling and the dopamine it evokes in the brains of betters undoubtedly helps solidify this very dangerous false idol to be cemented in so many psyches across the planet.

The NFL is one of the most prominent examples of this false idol, and in the United States, it is the greatest example. However, virtually all major sports contain the creation of false idols. For example, Major League Baseball games have two-minute and twenty-five-second breaks for nationally televised games and two-minute and five-second commercial breaks for local broadcasts (MLB.com, 2024). There are, hypothetically, an infinite amount of breaks that can cultivate false idols during a baseball game and the average game lasts about three hours. The National Hockey League has games that last around two and one-half hours. The actual time it takes to play a hockey game is sixty minutes with two twenty-minute intermissions. When one accounts for all of the stoppages and plays due to icing, penalties, and other infractions, commercials compose around a half-hour of the game. The National Basketball Association plays games with four twelve-minute quarters, and therefore, the whole game lasts 48 minutes. They get an additional fifteen minutes for halftime and that brings their total game length to an hour and three minutes. They also have many stoppages due to a wealth of infractions that tend to increase game length significantly. In total, they have more commercials, and the game lasts between a half-hour and forty-five minutes longer due to those commercials. However, like the NHL, their games tend to last two hours and thirty minutes.

In other words, the same basic virus infects the vast majority of sports, and the vast majority of sports serve as an attractive diversion for many of its fans. However, the false idols that are created in football dwarf the other three major sports in the United States combined. The same commercial virus does infect other sports like it infects football. However, because football has been able to attain widespread popularity since the inception of the NFL in 1920, it has been co-opted. It has been co-opted because it is the greatest vehicle to distract the people who are watching it.

Sports have a majesty and intensity that few other activities in our existence have or even come close to having. Millions of people play sports every day and, while it varies widely across age groups, all age groups enjoy and engage in sports. They provide relief, exercise, enjoyment, competition, and excitement in many ways.

Watching experts play sports can be as exhilarating and enthralling as playing them. Putting on the colors of our favorite team from our favorite city and with the numbers of our favorite player is something that creates identity, enjoyment, and tremendous passion that helps us to transcend the pain in our own lives. Many of you who are reading these words can probably think of a time when sports were something very dear and very important to your existence. This could be because it helped you bond with a friend or meet new friends, to feel part of the team or to feel the joy of being the antagonist against your friends who loved other teams. There is no doubt that sports are magical and while on paper they seem so simple, they take on an immense and exhilarating life of their own once the ball is picked up or that great team is being watched.

However, there are always nefarious forces that can see how much we love our sports. And those nefarious forces can use our interests, zeal, and adoration for self-interested means and ends. For the advertisers, this is to gain our hard-earned monies. Their ads are psychologically well-researched and are often extremely manipulative and executed. Every time you see a young person wearing the jersey and fantasizing about being their favorite player, there is a marketing opportunity. Advertisers create an atmosphere wherein we strive to be something we are not because we're made to feel like we should be something we are not. This hurts our psychological composition by pulling us away from who we are. The schism of self is subtle. But it is real and it is effective at altering how we think about the world, how we think about each other, and how we think about ourselves.

There is another entity that benefits from our distraction and the creation of false idols in sports. This entity is at least as old as Rome itself. While the Coliseum was originally created to revitalize Rome and create a vast entertainment source, it quickly became something else. It became a way to distract people and keep their attention over here while the leaders of Rome were engaged in corruption elsewhere. It is the inception of the distraction that power, or politics, often uses to quell and pacify while they engage in corrupt activities that destroy or deny what is good for the people.

Preserving the greatness of sports while not allowing them to be manipulated to rob us of what matters has been something that every civilization has likely struggled with to some extent from the time of the Romans to the present day. Finding a way to break free of the metaphorical chains that sports and entertainment often create seems vital for us to progress.

Chapter 5

Politics

The philosopher, linguist, and social critic Noam Chomsky, in his book *Who Rules the World* (2016), wrote, "As long as the general population is passive, apathetic, and diverted to consumerism or the hatred of the vulnerable, then the powerful can do as they please, and those who survive will be left to contemplate the outcome" (p. 56).

The diversion that Chomsky notes is pervasive and subtly infects almost every aspect of our society. However, it is undeniable that this social control and the deleterious effects that come with it are inherent in our political system. Our politicians are the epicenters of power in our society and that power should be derived directly from where it emanates from: the people. The people should, theoretically, have well-determined goals and aspirations for the politicians to follow. Those goals and aspirations should be in their own interest and should be carried out by the elected representatives who, ideally, should serve the role of puppet for the people's will.

However, this is not the case. Instead, our politicians tend to dabble in distraction. As in the realm of sports in the previous chapter, the realm of politics ascertains great benefit from the creation of false idols. As Chomsky noted, distraction is the only strategy to divert our attention from what matters. Juvenal recognized this over two thousand years ago and it had the same truth then that it does now. The strategy of the elites and especially of the politicians who are guided by the elites, is to distract us. It is no longer "bread and circuses" that serve as our distraction. Instead, it is a continuous loop of red herrings in which we get lost. We often think we care about so much that we forget the egregious and despicable wrongs that are being done subtly and quietly in every moment of every day by the antagonists of our power structure: the politicians.

Do you remember the 1997 movie, *Wag the Dog*? If not, here's the basic plot. The president of the United States is caught coming on to an underage girl in the Oval Office just before his election. Instead of facing the issue head-on, the president and his team create a fictional war in Albania in order to distract the public from the scandal. They elaborately create a theme song, fake footage of the war, and, in essence, create an entirely believable distraction in terms of turning the volume down on the president's sexual indiscretions.

This movie is presented as a comedy. The fact that the president is creating a fake war to distract the public is written in a way that does make us laugh. However, it is a dark comedy and it is a satire much in the same way that Juvenal's *Satires* were written.

Wag the Dog was a prophetic story, too. It was released two months before Bill Clinton's affair with Monica Lewinsky became public. The two narratives were eerily similar. What was more alarming than the affair was that Bill Clinton proceeded to bomb the Al-Shifa pharmaceutical factory in Sudan in August… just seven months after the scandal occurred (Barletta, 1998). He then proceeded to bomb Iraq during his impeachment trial over the scandal in December of the same year (Clines and Myers, 1998). This may have been a distraction at its zenith in a political context. It is far from the only time a politician used distraction to set the agenda onto something that will be advantageous for him or her politically. However, it is a particularly poignant example of the possible concept of distraction in a political context. Of particular note should be the blatant disregard for human life and the attempt to change the news cycle from one story to another. In other words, the politician, and in this case, the President, seemed to rather put human beings in harm's way and even allow them to die so that the constituents they serve are "looking over there" rather than paying attention to what is hurting them politically.

Who can deny that this has become the norm in American politics and politics around the world? In some ways, it can be argued that the entire arena of politics has become one large distraction. This is not a new concept. It has been in existence for some time. However, it is hard to refute that it is getting worse with each and every passing day.

Since the advent of social media, this distraction has worsened significantly. Social media should, in theory, greatly improve our knowledge and political acumen by the fact that it connects us to each other and it helps make news readily available to us. However, these were not the findings that researchers have found. In a study in 2019 by Lee and Xenos that surveyed two of the more recent American elections, the authors examined how political and social media use and general social media use affected and influenced the political knowledge that was ascertained. In both elections, the authors concluded that social media use does nothing significant to increase political knowledge. All of that information and all of that ease of access that was never available to our ancestors does nothing to make us a more enlightened populace who are ready to vote for our interests. Instead, it hurts us. The researchers actually concluded that general social media usage actually negatively impacts our political knowledge. Perhaps even more frightening, the article notes that two thirds of individuals in the United States get their news from this very source that doesn't give them any knowledge or accurate news.

In other words, social media started off as a bright light that could help advance democracy. However, once the forces of power and influence that have corrupted every aspect of our democracy from the inception of its existence got their hands on it, it has become just another bread and circus for us to find false idols and erroneous red herrings. It went from having the potential to enrich to becoming the vehicle to distract. And this is where it sits today, as a thorn in the side of American democracy and democracy all over the world.

This disturbing and tragic trend in the usage of social media is not by any means solely relegated to being an American phenomenon. On May 22, 2022, authors Barberá et al. published a journal article entitled, *Distract and Divert: How World Leaders Use Social Media during Contentious Politics.* They analyzed world leader's communication and habits through a variety of social media outlets. They found that world leaders extremely often used social media to shift the conversation from domestic issues to foreign policy anytime there was social unrest. In other words, every time the position was at risk, they used social media to distract the population they served in order to retain their position and improve the social rankings amongst the populace. They distracted the people they serve in order to take the light off of something they did not want them to see or dwell on. Perhaps even more disturbing, this was especially done during elections and the time right before an election.

Many of us probably do this with our children. There is little doubt that we can all remember a time when we distracted our children from pain by offering them something else that they were interested in or wanted. If we have not done this with our own children, surely we can remember a time when our parents did this with us. "I'm so sorry that happened to you," the parent says to her son as the son winces in pain due to his skinned knee as it is bleeding and she is putting on a bandage. "How about I make you that apple pie you always love so much and we can sit and watch a movie together?" It is cute and helpful and endearing when a caregiver distracts the child from their pain. This is because, in these cases, the motive is pure and good. The parent distracts as a method of pain management.

However, the politician distracts as a method of self-enrichment. This self-enrichment is most often financial or an attempt to salvage their career, which can also be seen as financial. It is this self-enrichment that lies at the core of the destruction of democracy. It is this self-enrichment that creates an atmosphere of deception that destroys the enlightenment that is necessary for the citizenry to elect and sustain political figures that truly represent them. Politicians should be experts in creating meaningful change in the lives of their constituents. However, social media, as well as many other distractions, enables them to create a career around becoming experts in self-deception.

Who exhibits this more than Donald Trump? Distraction is the foundation of his quest for and claims to power. Researchers from Bristol University analyzed Donald Trump's use of social media during the Russian Probe that investigated whether his campaign communicated with Russia in an attempt to help him get elected president. They compared those results to his regular output on social media. They found that the more the probe was covered, the more Mr. Trump tweeted about things for which he had a modicum of support from his constituency in the United States. Immigration policy, a keystone issue for Trump, was one such issue that he used consistently and incessantly to distract the public from any of the headlines regarding the possible collusion between him and the Russian government to get him elected. As a result, every time there was negative news in the American public about him that related to the Russian probe, it got less coverage. He made sure that his presidential tweets stole much of the coverage that the Russian probe would've gotten otherwise.

There is unequivocally no better example of the use of distraction by utilizing social media than Trump's January 6th insurrection to remain in power.

Social media has been the basis by which Donald Trump has risen to much of his power. No politician in American history has ever utilized social media to distract in a way that Trump has. The United States Presidential election was held on November 3, 2020. Donald Trump faced Joe Biden. The final tally in the popular vote was 81,283,501 for Joe Biden and 74,223,975 for Donald Trump. The electoral vote, which very sadly continues to be the most important vote in the United States, ended with 306 electoral votes for Joe Biden and 232 for Donald Trump. (Federal Election Commission, 2022).

No rational human being could look at the number 81,283,501 and say it is in any way lesser than the number 74,223,975. This is the popular vote and this is the most representative number of how many individuals wanted Joe Biden to be president in comparison to Donald Trump. It is 9.5% higher.

However, that's not how the framers of the Constitution created our democracy. They put in a safeguard called the Electoral College that essentially mitigates the concept of popular vote. Therefore, the president is determined by the electoral vote. In this tally, Joe Biden received seventy-four more electoral votes. Joe Biden won the popular vote and won the electoral vote. Enough said, right?

Wrong. Donald Trump claimed the votes were fraudulently counted, and based on that so-called fraudulent account, he claimed that he was still president. There was not an iota of evidence that suggested this was a true statement.

In other words, he used distraction to undermine truth. He used social media to do this throughout his presidency, and he used his podium to do it both throughout his presidency and especially on election night.

But the distraction did not end there. Despite the utter lack of evidence to support an absurd claim that undermined democracy across not only the country but the world, he continued on. He continued to distract by using social media and calling on two thousand of his most dedicated and most mindless followers to run like lemmings to the capital and sacrifice themselves for his distractions. And they did. He distracted the country with one of many false claims during his presidency and distracted his supporters into believing that the only way to support their country was to sacrifice themselves for his lies. These distractions, like Clinton's distractions, resulted in people dying. However, these distractions also resulted in the decay of one of the greatest concepts in the history of humanity: democracy.

His supporters saw and continue to see him as a false idol. His active cultivation of himself as a false idol creates a widespread fog of distraction that enables him to distract by any means necessary so that he can enrich his self-concept in a way that has not been seen since the days of dictatorial monarchs. And he has done all of it by sitting at a desk and, typing lies, distractions, and creating a persona that enables him to be a false idol for the masses. His primary weapon has been social media.

What is more worrisome is that other world leaders are following the same social media trend of distraction. According to Barberá and Zeitzoff (2017), by the end of 2014, more than 76% of the leaders of the world's countries utilize social media. Seventy-six percent. This was in the time before Trump and his rampant abuse of social media and manipulation of social media to help him mitigate democracy. This number is sure to only rise, and in its rising, one can expect the abuses of social media will continue to abound as a distraction for the people.

Social media is not the only form of self-deception that politicians utilize to distract. Russia's dictator, Vladimir Putin, readily embraces increases in his influence over many parts of Russian life but, especially the state media. He, like other corrupt leaders, uses state media to silence anyone who defies their authority or their message. They also use state media to promote their own falsehoods much like Donald Trump. However, war is used equally and often as a diversionary tactic to keep people either "in their place" or distracted. The distraction of war is in the playbook of every corrupt leader.

This concept is called diversionary foreign policy. This is the concept that was touched on regarding Bill Clinton's military action that distracted the public from his sexual pursuits. Smith (1996) describes the concept of diversionary foreign policy as, "foreign policies designed to help a government retain power" (p. 133). Using this definition, any foreign-policy interaction that benefits presidents, czars, dictators, or rulers of any kind by distracting the public is a form of diversionary foreign policy. When viewed from this lens, it becomes glaringly obvious that this mode of "bread and circuses" is used constantly by our leaders to focus our attention on anything but what they want us to focus our attention. This practice is widespread and constant and is amongst the premier forms of distraction. Let's examine just a few of the many examples of this antidemocratic and immoral practice around the world.

The French Revolutionary Wars of 1792 were fought after the French government had just created a National Assembly. This National Assembly was formed to replace the long-standing French monarchy consisting of its current monarch, King Louis XVI. The National Assembly needed a way to distract the people from the drama, and what could possibly be a greater distraction than a foreign war? This is how the French Revolutionary Wars began. The Assembly first declared a war on Austria and then on Prussia. It was purely a distraction. It was a diversionary foreign policy (Cashman, 1999).

In March of 2014, Vladimir Putin ordered Russian troops to invade and take over the Crimean Peninsula from Ukraine. According to Theiler of the *Journal Security Studies* (2017), the Russian act of foreign policy, "increased national pride among Russians while support for Vladimir Putin rose dramatically, and they suggest that the two processes were causally linked" (p. 318).

There are many other examples of diversionary foreign policy. However, it is important to note that diversionary foreign policy is a concept that is very strongly contested in certain circles. Why is something so obvious contested? It's contested because it is not empirically provable. In other words, no one can say definitively that the National Assembly in France started that war in order to create an atmosphere wherein the country could all rally behind the new government. The motives of the Assembly could have been entirely different. Put simply, motives are subjective and personal and are very difficult to prove.

We know this, however. Anyone who has ever gotten summoned for jury duty knows that we are often called to take our best and educated guess at someone else's motives. It is one of the pillars of our very legal system… a legal system that has much of its foundation as far back as ancient Rome. In any criminal case, we are legally obligated to examine and attempt to understand the motives of both defendants and plaintiffs. We are asked to use our best judgment based on a preponderance of the evidence to understand and make our best conjectures as to why and how one individual did something to another. These judgments are binding and can result in the incarceration of, and, in some cases, the death of other human beings. This is almost universally accepted as appropriate and important to a functioning legal system in the United States.

Therefore, the fact that diversionary foreign policy isn't contested seems disturbing. Just as we use a preponderance of the evidence to make our best guesses when determining the fate of someone's life in the courtroom, we are most certainly entitled to use that same preponderance of evidence to make our best guesses when determining the motives of people we elect. Do we ever understand the full picture? Absolutely not. We were never in the rooms and certainly could not have understood all of the variables that went into their decisions to start any wars. However, we most certainly can make broad assumptions about the human behavior of others. We do this each and every day with a tremendous amount of zeal and interest as a necessity to make our way through our lives intelligently. There is no reason that any politician should be exempt from the same rule we use for strangers or our loved ones. Given this preponderance of the evidence, it becomes clear that leaders currently and always have used their power to divert our attention from a wide variety of other issues. It becomes abundantly clear that diversionary foreign policy is amongst the greatest tools for leaders to defy democracy and implore us to do and focus on what they want us to focus on.

War is obviously horrific and amongst the worst actions that any leader can take if it is unprovoked and unmerited. However, it is fairly obvious that leaders are well aware of how much war can force the populace to repress any anger they are feeling about the government or any plight in their lives that the government may be able to ameliorate. Therefore, diversionary foreign policy has several effects on the populace. First, it most certainly has the effect of the state saying, "look at that," in a way that we are forced to divert our attention from one issue to another. However, the diversion does not stop there. The diversion quickly becomes repression. Oxford Learner's Dictionary defines a patriot as, "a person who loves the country and who is ready to defend it against an enemy" (para. 1). Given this definition, it would be unpatriotic to question our government during any war, especially when we can't absolutely prove the motives for that war, right? This is the cultural sentiment that forces the strangulation of democracy and coerced loyalty. We are presented a situation wherein we will feel like cultural outcasts and traitors if we question any war that our nation launches. Herein lies the complacency. We don't have all the facts and to question the facts is considered unpatriotic. Therefore, we must give our leaders the benefit of the doubt. This is the second major byproduct of all diversionary foreign policy moves: deference.

The false idol in diversionary foreign policy becomes the leaders themselves. We are made to feel that we cannot question the leader in times of immediacy, and all other concerns of the Republic, including our own economic, mental, and physical well-being, become subservient to the leader and their usurpation of power. This form of false idol used by politicians is quite strong and quite effective. However, there is yet another way that politicians create these false idols to distract and divide.

Juvenal discussed circuses, which are entertainment. However, he also mentioned bread. Bread is economics. Economics pervades every aspect of every civilization that has ever lived. No one can be alive and avoid the long arm of economics. Therefore, there is no easier target to use for distraction than by economics.

According to Merriam-Webster's Dictionary, economics is, "a social science concerned chiefly with description and analysis of the production, distribution, and consumption of goods and services" (para. 1). In other words, it is the study of the distribution of wealth in a given society and how that distribution of wealth effects that society. The discipline of economics is typically traced back to the year 1776. This is when Adam Smith published his famous economic treaties, *The Wealth of Nations.* This is when capitalism was officially born out of its feudal and mercantile predecessors. After Smith, a variety of economic critics began commenting on the system of capitalism and how this system affects individuals who live within it. John Stuart Mill, David Ricardo, Thomas Robert Malthus, and others were among the first to create a study of how the organization of wealth in a society affects the distribution of goods and the very well-being and overall health of that society. (Heilbroner, 1999).

However, no economist was more critical of this new system than Karl Marx. He was highly critical of the exploitation and the imbalance between the bourgeoisie (haves) and the proletariat (have-nots). Marx conceived of a concept implicit in the capitalist system, which is, 'class consciousness.' He discussed how the classes that form due to socioeconomic status slowly become aware of the exploitation they are experiencing from the classes above them. This class consciousness leads to conflict. (Heilbroner, 1999).

Antonio Gramsci was a philosopher and a Marx acolyte who further developed some of Marx's concepts. He discusses the concept of cultural hegemony. Cultural hegemony is the ruling classes' (bourgeoisie) manipulation of the values in society so as to create the dominant cultural worldview in that society. In other words, he argued that the politicians and the wealthy will create a worldview that becomes *the worldview* of a capitalist society. It is the cultural dominance of the wealthy and those who are in power to set the agenda for the culture for everyone. (Flint and Taylor, 2018).

The concept of hegemony is crucial to the concept of "bread and circuses" and the way politicians use economic culture to distract. Cultural distraction is amongst if not the single most effective tool to create diversion and distraction that destroys any democracy.

To illustrate this, we need not look any further than our own families and our own lives. We are all victims of hegemony. It starts with our parents and their cultural dominance in the household in which we grew up. This is a microcosm of the overall concept of hegemony. Our parents set a family culture. That culture may include an irate and dominant Dad who sets the agenda and dominates almost all norms and conditions of behavior. Or, it may include a Mom who is very particular about how she wants things and has an overwhelming amount of love to spread across the family. There are an endless amount of variations in family culture, and as a therapist, I am all too privy to this fact. The point is that whoever serves as the "ruling class" in the family sets the culture of that family. Whoever sets the culture of that family has a great deal of power over how the family thinks and to get us to believe what they want us to believe.

The vast majority of psychoanalytic analysis is dedicated to the basic premise that what happens in our developmental years affects us later in our lives. In the microcosm I am presenting, I am using the same premise. Our dictatorial dad creates cultural norms for behavior that changes the way we think and interact with the world for many years to come. In fact, for many of us, those cultural norms that dad or mom or grandma set will stay with us and affect the way we act and behave throughout our lives. Think about your own life. How many aspects of your behavior have been affected because your mom or dad or brother or sister did them growing up? We all have been incredibly influenced by the culture of our past.

It is no different on a grander scale. Obviously, and in general, no one has the effect on us that our early caregivers had. However, culture erupts as a new parental unit, generally in our teenage years, and that new parental unit creates a new culture that often differs from moms or dads or grandma's culture. Being the herd animal that we can often be, society then becomes a new sort of parent. This new parent mandates the cultural mores, beliefs, and norms for suitable behavior in a similar way to the mandated culture of our family. Whereas our family culture has specific sanctions that usually involve the withholding of emotions, punishments for aberrant behavior, and so forth, society uses similar means to condition and cultivate the behavioral ends it wants.

No, society is not our surrogate parent. However, it serves as an entity that rises to the level of one for many of us. It tells us how to behave and what to do in the same ways that our parents did. It informs us how you dress, what you care about, where you go, how you live, and presents a litany of other behavioral norms that have very specific parameters to which we must adhere.

Who leads this society? Who creates these norms and concepts of behavior and has the ability to distract us? That question is far more complex. There is obviously not one person who does it the way our caretaker, mom or dad, does it when we are growing up. Rather, it is a large and complex web of institutions, individuals, and leaders who create these norms and concepts of behavior. Unlike the family unit, there is not one single person that can be pointed to in order to describe responsibility. It is very subjective because most of us tend to listen to different entities in society. However, there is one thing that is indisputable. Just as Marx and Gramsci foretold, the individuals with the power, that is, those who have found themselves on the most advantageous levels of the economic ladder, are the ones who make the rules. It is the powerful... the wealthy, and the elite who are able to set many of the cultural standards for any given society. In the analogy I have created, the upper classes serve as the new parents to set the culture and the mores for the masses. It is not by dictatorial decree, but rather by preying on our herd instinct. The primary way that the concepts and dictates are abided by is by preying on our desires not to be outside of the norm. This is because, for many, being different or marching to the beat of a different drummer has long been among the hardest achievements for human beings to achieve. Because we don't want to be left out, we listen. Therefore, the power structures simply set the new trend, and one group follows. After one group follows, more groups follow. It is not long before everyone feels that they have to follow so as not to risk the single greatest terror that any human being could ever experience: ostracism!

We have now identified the cycle of economic diversion. It exists at this moment as you read this, and it will exist at least as long as capitalism serves as the primary economic modality of our society. Let's examine some examples of how this mechanism is working right now in contemporary society.

To understand economic diversion, we must understand economic culture. Culture is the wellspring of the herd instinct, and it is culture that serves as the oil that keeps the economic engine of the United States or any country running. Culture is fluid in that it can change and there are many different influences that come together to create it. It is the omnipotent source that drives the herd, and therefore, it can be a tremendous asset to democracy or other systems in society or, alternatively, it can be the death toll to virtually any system in society. Therefore, the utmost attention must be given to what may seem like almighty culture and its tremendous effect on the behavior of human beings.

Dr. Weaver of Maxwell Air University in Montgomery, Alabama, demonstrates one way that culture, and particularly economic culture, was born in the United States. He discusses how, in the 1700s and 1800s, there was extremely little economic mobility in Europe. The constriction of economic mobility and the fact that all of culture was restrained by this constriction resulted in a populace who were willing to take chances to achieve a better material existence. They set sail for this new and free country called America, knowing that at least 20% of them – one in five – would not survive the voyage. (Weaver, 1999).

This, he argues, was the inception of the American cultural belief in risk-taking. This created a culture wherein one was encouraged to take risks to better their economic existence and, therefore to better their existence in general. Dr. Weaver exhibits how this affected the rest of American culture. This cultural precedent of taking an enormous risk exhibits itself in the very concept of the American Dream, which was based on the concept of economic advancement and upward mobility and hard work. These concepts, which were heavily influenced by the Protestant belief system, set and created an economic culture based on risk, economic mobility, hard work, self-reliance, and many other creeds and belief systems. (Weaver, 1999).

These were the economic values that were brought to this country by the immigrants who first came. These values still exist today in every way and can be seen in every thread of the fabric of our culture. They are inescapable, just as our family culture was inescapable when we were born. These values are pervasive and intensely influential throughout our culture and our lives. They affect the well-being of millions of people every day and have a tremendous impact on how people feel about themselves, how people feel about others, and the decisions that they make in all facets of their lives.

But how can this be? The immigrants who came over and set the foundation for these conceptions and values are long gone. Their contributions to the United States were made hundreds of years ago, and over those hundreds of years, culture should have changed, right?

It should have. And it has, to some extent. The concept of self-reliance is still widely embraced by most of the population, however, the notion of dependence and reliance on the community is not held in the same high esteem that it was two hundred years ago and most certainly even sixty or seventy years ago. But by and large, the American economic value system has remained the same. Even regarding the value of self-reliance, there are still major parts of the public who don't believe in the concept of reliance on the greater society economically or in any other way to this day. So, while there is some movement in values and the operationalizing of those values in the United States, these basic and original values set two hundred and three hundred years ago have remained static.

This is one clear example of how economic culture in the United States was created, augmented, and has endured from its inception until today. However, within the skeleton of this framework of values, there is a wealth of other beliefs, cultural frameworks, and values that pervade our lives. These values are not maintained based on homage to individuals who existed three hundred years ago. They are actively cultivated and nurtured by our society each and every day.

German sociologist and political economist Max Weber suggested other ways in which our economic culture and values were created and endured. In his book, *The Protestant Ethic and the Spirit of Capitalism*, Weber (2003) argued that the Protestant work ethic was a major factor in the rise and spread of capitalism. The major factor that it played illustrates this constant shaping of culture through beliefs. The dominant Protestant culture embraced and promoted capitalist ideals, and that hegemonic force was integral in the spread of the capitalist ideology.

The cultivation of these values creates paradigms, structures, creeds, and behaviors that we are to live by if we are to be "normal" and not ostracized in society. These values are manipulated and utilized by those with the motives to do so in order to distract. If we are too busy equating our self-worth with wealth, we may forget that a massive 12.6% of our neighbors were living in poverty in the United States in 2022 (Benson, 2023). Keep in mind for 2022 the poverty level was a completely unlivable and absurdly low $12,590 (U.S. Department of Health and Human Services, 2022). If we are fixated on the delusion that we can be the next "great" entrepreneur who can make millions per year if we just worked a little later and a little harder, we may forget that nearly 29% of the individuals in the United States are considered 'lower class' and, in 2018 numbers, has a median income of just $25,654 (Elkins, 2019).

As noted, there is no one person or one entity that is responsible for constantly propagating a culture that is self-fulfilling. However, there are many entities who want to continue to preach values that run against the very values of the people who accept them. Any time there is a self-interest involved in the creation of these values, these overwhelming negative political entities exist. The system of distraction serves to keep the power structure stable and empower the few while we continue to seek to become something that we are not and will never be. We are left in a constant state of desire and self-loathing, and the power structure is sustained by a constant state of avarice and the desire for power. This cycle is perpetuated, and in this perpetuation, it leaves a wake of pained psyches, wounded egos, and an utter lack of the sense of self that is needed to become an authentic, good, and true human being.

Any value system that rivaled the value system of the groups who bask in power, wealth, and self-interest is eliminated. The United States was largely created by individuals who ascribed to the Christian religion. Some of the core values of Christianity are loving your neighbor as you would yourself, embracing poverty and focusing on what's truly important, loving those who are downtrodden or outcasts in society, endlessly forgiving, endless humility, and a devotion to God, a power far greater than yourself. These values run in direct contrast to the economic values described in this chapter. Therefore, they are continuing to be slowly but surely eroded and purged from a system that worships at the altar of the opposite values. There have been other value systems that have challenged the economic value system, but they are all put aside, purged, and disregarded. The power that creates this disregard is, as always, the herd instinct, which serves as a power stronger in the human heart than self-interest, will, or anything in between.

German philosopher and political theorist Hannah Arendt, in her essay, "Personal Responsibility under Dictatorship," discussed the concept of voluntarily complying with a dictatorial and unfair entity. She considered those who have the courage to refuse to comply with injustice and found that those people have the ability to make judgments for themselves. In other words, they followed their own conscience and belief system rather than false idols. She said they had the courage to refuse to comply, "...because they asked themselves to what extent they would still be able to live in peace with themselves after having committed certain deeds" (Tömmel and Passerin d'Entreves, 2024, sec. 6.3).

We, too, are asked whether we will be able to live in peace with ourselves as we make our decisions regarding how we engage with our politicians and our political system in general. We also have a personal responsibility to do what we see as right rather than acquiesce to the constant distractions and diversions that those in power so often use.

Whether it is in economics, foreign policy, social media, or an endless amount of other issues, distraction is the tool that politicians and other individuals in power use to maintain their power. This concept is probably as old as human beings, and the distraction that is being used pervades our world and has a direct and immensely negative impact on our society as a whole. The question of whether we can awake from our collective slumber and identify what is occurring for what it is remains unanswered. The only certainty for now is that the recipe works, and whether it was in ancient Rome or in the contemporary United States, this version of "bread and circuses" will continue to be used until we don't allow it to be used anymore.

One of the ways for the people to reject the bread and circuses that are pacifying us can be through the arts. Art, music, and literature have always been beacons of light for humanity that have the propensity to not only unite us but also bring social change to our politics and economics that often fail to deliver social justice. Let's next examine how the concept of false idols has affected the arts.

Chapter 6

Art, Music, Literature

The twentieth-century poet, critic, and editor Ezra Pound wrote in *Literary Essays* (1968), "Artists are the antenna of the race, but the bullet-headed many will never learn to trust their great artists" (p.58). Ezra Pound had an enormous influence on twentieth-century literature largely due to his unique poetry as well as his support and influence over writers such as T. S. Eliot, James Joyce, W. B. Yeats, Ernest Hemingway, Robert Frost, and many others. While Pound had very eccentric and questionable political views, his artistic and literary views and sense were remarkable and changed the way the world viewed art and literature.

The fact that he characterized artists as the "antenna of the race" is a tremendous statement. He saw art as a vehicle through which society progressed. An antenna on any living thing enables that living thing to feel its way through the world and detect air, motion, and vibration. Furthermore, it allows it to touch, smell, and taste. Just think of what senses mean to us. Without being able to touch, smell, or taste, detect air, detect motion, or feel vibration, we would be almost wholly reliant on our only other two senses, sight and sound. Because many entities that have antennae generally do not have an excellent sense of sight or sound, you could say that their antenna is the only way they can successfully navigate the world.

This is what Ezra Pound is saying that art and the artist serve as for humanity. He is saying that artists provide for us with a framework by which we can successfully navigate the world around us. Who can refute the wisdom of Pound's words? Everyone is influenced by art. Art is a widely inclusive term that includes drawing, painting, film, sculpting, photography, sculpture, literature, dance, music, and so many other modes of human expression.

Art is more widely defined, according to Oxford English Dictionary (2024), as "the expression or application of human creative skill and imagination, typically in a visual form such as painting or sculpting, producing works to be appreciated primarily for their beauty or emotional power" (para. 2). In his book *What is Art* (2000), Leo Tolstoy, the great writer, moralist, and philosopher, and a contemporary of Pound, defined art as anything that communicates emotion. He wrote, "Art begins when one person, with the object of joining another or others to himself in one and the same feeling, expresses that feeling by certain external indications" (p.48). While these are all excellent definitions, for the purposes of this chapter, art will be defined simply as self-expression. Self-expression can be solitary, but when it is produced in a way that is available and can affect the masses, it can be, as Pound said, the divining rod or guidestick for the human race.

As proof of this thesis, one only has to look at art's effect on humanity in all its forms. In an article written by Sherman and Morissey (2017), the authors argue for art's ability to increase one's self-knowledge while simultaneously communicating in a profound way with other people. They review its unique ability to challenge our perceptions and conceptions about the world while simultaneously encouraging personal growth. Art does all of these things and it is unique in its ability to move and inspire and change us. Art moves far beyond aesthetic pleasure alone and most epistemological inquiry into art leaves out its social and political ramifications. It is undeniably an active social practice that redefines our sense of selves and also who we are as a community.

Art is not new to humanity. It is not something that solely occurred after Gutenberg's printing press but rather has been with us since the inception of our existence. As Sanjay Jangid, Dean of Animation and Design at Chitkara University notes, "Ancient artists showcased their daily lives in the form of cave paintings and petroglyphs in Bhimbhetka, Venus of Berekhat Ram, and others around the world" (Jangid, 2022). There is no doubt that these cave paintings were seen as expressive outlets from the start. These cave paintings, in a way, were analogous to the first books, the first singers, the first musicians, in short, the first artists who served as antennae for the rest of us to empathize, understand ourselves, and better navigate the difficulty of our lives.

There are almost endless examples to use in between the cave paintings of our ancient ancestors to the catchy jingles of our current pop music stars. For instance, the shaking hips and sensuous ways that Elvis sang as he sang and danced to the black music that he heard as a young man changed not only popular music but all of American culture forever.

However, let's examine this phenomenon in regard to literature. Geoffrey Chaucer wrote *The Canterbury Tales,* which was a major narrative poem in the 1300s (Chaucer, 2005). It, along with his other works, greatly affected and changed English literature forever. Of particular note, was the fact that Chaucer decided to write in English, rather than the Latin or French, which was very popular at the time. This changed the English language forever and promoted it in a way that helped its survival immensely. He had such an enormous impact that a fellow poet of his day, Thomas Hoccleve, stated that he was the, "the firste fyndere of our fair langage," meaning, "the first founder of our fair language" (Simpson, 2023, p. 28).

Shakespeare was an immense admirer of Chaucer. In Shakespeare's Play *Two Noble Kingsman,* he gives Chaucer the credit for the play, and it is clear from this alone that he thought highly of his predecessor. Like Chaucer, the writing of Shakespeare has also had an immense impact on the development of the English language as well as on our culture and the way we think about the world.

Like Chaucer, Shakespeare revolutionized the English language. It was only after Shakespeare that the language had standard grammatical rules. This was largely because his works were so widely read, and due to their prevalence, their influence took root in the minds of the English people. Many of Shakespeare's words and phrases were used so widely in the vernacular of England that he created many words in his plays and redefined many others (Lynch, 2007). His influence on the way that English was understood, seen, and read was more dramatic than any other writer in human history. Shakespeare, like Chaucer, and many other great writers, left an artistic imprint on humanity that has prevailed and deeply affected the way we live. This is the power of art to affect culture. It can be seen in literature, in music, in painting, and in virtually any other mode of self-expression and expulsion of human emotion that we call art.

Therefore, the importance of art in all its forms to any society is obvious. Art connects us and frees us and creates an atmosphere wherein we can grow mentally, emotionally, and morally. It is, as Pound stated, part of what enables us to continue to feel our way forward as we navigate our existence and it has a tremendous power over us.

Since this is the case, it follows that art must be completely free in any given society. Any society which hosts the censorship of artistic discretion will intrinsically trip and falter. UNESCO, or the United Nations Educational, Scientific and Cultural Organization, defines artistic expression as, "the freedom to imagine, create and distribute diverse cultural expressions free of governmental censorship, political interference or the pressures of non-state actors" (UNESCO, 2017). In other words, in order for art to contribute the greatness that it does to any given society, that society must not encumber or prohibit its expression through censorship in all of its forms.

FreedomHouse.org is a nonprofit and nonpartisan organization whose sole purpose is to help create a world where all are free. They do so primarily by researching and presenting information on the status of freedom in the world. In 2017, they created a world ranking system that gauges how countries create atmospheres that contain the most freedom of expression. The representation of governmentally allowed expression presents a dreary picture, to say the least. A very significant part of the world and its many countries live under cultures and laws that create an atmosphere wherein expression is muted and deterred on many levels. (Freedomhouse.org, 2023).

Most of the Western world is not a part of this artistic censorship. North America, Europe, South America, and many other places in the Western Hemisphere are extremely open and welcoming to artistic expression. There are also many places in the East, such as Australia, India, Mongolia, and others that received very high rankings for allowing and creating an atmosphere that cultivates artistic expression. This artistic expression is sometimes codified in some kind of legal statute, such as a constitution. For example, the United States contains the First Amendment which guarantees freedom of speech and prohibits the government from censoring free speech, which is the guarantee against the prohibition of artistic expression. Other countries codify the right to artistic expression in a more direct way. For example, Germany and Sweden and France all have specifically created laws that foster an atmosphere of free and open artistic expression that preserves this fundamental and elemental right for all of the people that these countries govern. (Freedomhouse.org, 2023).

The laws that have been created by the society and the open artistic expression that they claim to foster are undeniably large and important steps toward the creation of an open and artistically free society. However, the fact that a law was written has never made something a reality in itself. From prohibition to civil rights to speeding, a law is only as good as its widespread acceptance, agreement, and enforcement. Laws create an atmosphere of psychological security but unless they are widely agreed-upon and enforced, they are only as good as the paper that the lawmakers wrote them on.

In addition to communal consent, laws are affected by a wealth of other dependent variables. Martin Luther King famously said, "It's all right to tell a man to lift himself by his own bootstraps, but it is cruel jest to say to a bootless man that he ought to lift himself by his own bootstraps" (Logsdon, 2024, para. 32). King openly acknowledges the concept that is morally acceptable to ask someone to act in a certain way. This request would logically be acceptable to both the government and fellow human beings. However, he makes it clear that it is objectionable to ask someone who cannot possibly do something to do that very thing. In fact, it is clearly immoral to do so.

Using this logic, the laws that create an atmosphere where artistic expression is free and open are good and necessary in themselves. However, unless the population has the resources to create artistic expression and an unfettered way, the laws become less effective to say the least. Artistic expression only becomes meaningful if it can be attained by the masses in a way that is unfettered by any influence.

To be fair, it is culturally and societally impossible to create art devoid of any cultural or environmental influence. In fact, it would destroy much of the very foundation that art rests upon to take away the environmental factors that create an atmosphere for its existence. Art, in many ways, is a reaction to the world around us and therefore, the world around us is imperative to influence that reaction. Walt Whitman's *Leaves of Grass* would be completely different if it were not for the Civil War and Abraham Lincoln and his humanistic adoration for the soldiers and the cause. John Steinbeck had to see the migrant workers and the tremendous plight they suffered just down the road from his house in Salinas, California, in order to be inspired to create *The Grapes of Wrath*. I would argue that with every great work of literature, there is an atmosphere that helped produce that work of literature in the artist's mind. The mind can produce great literature, painting, and so on under almost any circumstance… and especially oppression.

However, whatever great art is produced, whether by painting, literature, sculpting, music, and so on, is only as visible as society allows it to be visible. In today's society, there are gatekeepers of art who are generally deemed necessary to select and promote certain works of art while shielding other works of art from being seen. These are ultimately the censors of art in modern-day society. Art's mass production and societal acceptance are wholly dependent upon the individuals who get to decide what art is "good" and what art is not. They decide what art is acceptable not based on aesthetic pleasure or moral message or intellectual enrichment. Rather, the decision seems clearly made by what will garner the most financial remuneration for its mass production and publication. This is the yardstick by which art is truly censored and limited: what sells. All of the laws and efforts to create a free and open society wherein everyone can express themselves any way they want is idyllic and laudable in every way. However, it is our economic system that truly determines what art has value and can be heard or what art does not and should be censored.

Let's explore this concept with some of the great art that many cherish. Franz Kafka was virtually unknown during his lifetime and his works did not curry favor with the gatekeepers around him. Emily Dickinson, Claude Monet, Vincent van Gogh, Paul Gaugin, Edgar Allen Poe, Henry David Thoreau, and countless others were not truly accepted or appreciated in their time. None of them were able to pass through the gatekeepers of their day to gain the widespread acceptance that gave them the acclaim that they only garnered after their deaths.

Why? Why are some great artists appreciated and adored during their lifetime, while others never experience this appreciation? How many other artists created divinely wonderful works but were never considered and whose names we will never know?

Obviously, this is a multifaceted question, and the answers to these questions are both legion and sometimes unknowable. However, all these artists and so many more have definitely been marginalized during their lifetime due to the culture around them. In each case, it is both clear and obvious that the culture did not appreciate their genius. That appreciation is derived from the values of the culture. The values of the culture are largely derived from the false idols created by a faulty economic system.

For example, the gatekeepers who control mass media are those who are given the honor of choosing who is worthy to be brought to the light of society. Now, no one can know definitively their motives or the basis for the conceptions behind why they pick one work and not another. However, what we can know is that financial remuneration is a vital motive if not the primary motive. How do we know this?

Because according to an article by The Guardian in 2022, 90% of the financial markets for publishing are controlled by five publishing houses. Journalist Betsy Reed writes, "As such, they have great cultural and – if a book takes off – economic power" (Reed, 2022). In other words, just five companies determine 90% of the literature that is read by us in print. Those five companies wield an almost endless power to influence our culture. What are the values that guide the decisions of these five companies? No one can say. But, given the fact that they are all very much for-profit companies, one can assume that attaining profit is amongst the top of those values. The market in the current financial situation of each of the companies surely garners much of what is chosen for publication.

Imagine how many of the great authors would never have made the cut from these five companies and their value. Can you imagine the deep psychological insights of Shakespeare, the postmodern stream of consciousness of Virginia Woolf, the moral fortitude of Upton Sinclair, or the strong masculine and stoic overtones of Ernest Hemingway not being accepted for publication?

Financial well-being and current cultural trends become the false idols that censor art in the modern-day. The almighty "free market" that Adam Smith described makes art into a popularity contest rather than a quest for meaning and self-expression. This popularity contest creates cultural norms and beliefs to which we find ourselves aspiring and emulating even when they are against our own self-interest. To illustrate this, let's examine some of the genres and books that were the highest-selling in just the last year.

The best-selling books of every year are released and listed by *Publishers Weekly*. The top 10 highest-selling books for 2022 contained six books by the same author. All six books have the same overarching theme: romance. Each of the six very dominating works of literature are romantic novels that not only involve but are heavily dominated by the themes and concepts that any classic love story contains.

Most of us know the basics of a love story. Love stories are not particularly thought-provoking but rather, emotionally evocative. Most have one character who meets another character, and much of the prose is dedicated to the spark between them and the interpersonal taboos and relational variables that contribute to whether they will be together or won't be together. They are all different, but they'll have rising action, climax, and falling action that follow a reliable and predictable pattern. They belong to a genre of literature called escapist literature or escapist fiction. Books that have heavily romantic themes and plot points are universally known and widely overdone in the canon of English literature. This is not to say that they cannot be excellent reading in their own right. It is to say, however, that they provide an escape or distraction from the world around us.

Escapist fiction, according to Elisa Galgut of the Oxford Handbook Of Philosophy And Psychoanalysis (2019), is any fiction that provides a psychological escape from reality in the world around them by the work immersing the reader in a "new world" that the author creates. To be fair, much of great literature and great art temporarily psychologically delivers us from the reality around us. However, art does not necessarily have that primary goal. One of the key facets of escapist literature or fiction is that the primary goal is to create a world around us from which we can leave this one and enter that one. Hence, the name of escapist literature is an exceptionally well-given title.

It should be noted that romance is but one genre of English literature that is given the title of escapist literature. It should also be noted that literature is not the only art that can be called escapist. Any art can be escapist. In terms of any literature and film: fantasy, detective, horror, science fiction, thrillers, and spy novels or movies are all other genres that are escapist in nature.

If you think of your favorite books, chances are one of them is escapist literature. It's that book that you grab and crawl up on the couch and lose yourself in because it transports you to an exciting and wonderful world wherein you don't have to think about your own world of problems anymore. This concept can be very useful from a psychological standpoint, and it has its place in literature, film, and other arts.

Some might say, "isn't all literature escapist?" That is an argument that can be made, but there are distinct differences. Let's take an example from a story that everyone knows. Charles Dickens wrote fifteen novels in his life as well as a wide range of novellas. There is one novella that I am confident that most in the Western world have read or heard or watched in their life: *A Christmas Carol*. This is the story of Bob Cratchit, his family, and the unforgettable Ebenezer Scrooge. We watch how the very economically poor but morally rich Bob Cratchit has a transformative effect over the economically rich but morally poor Ebenezer Scrooge with a little bit of help from the supernatural.

What is the difference between a Christmas Carol and other escapist literature? Charles Dickens was not writing solely to entertain. He is not asking us to get so immersed in the lives of Scrooge and the Cratchits that we forget the deeper and greater meaning of his work. In other words, Dickens had a greater and deeper meaning to what he was writing. Dickens wrote a Christmas Carol after he visited a school called, "Field Lane Ragged School." This was a school provided for the street children of London. The abuses and mistreatment that he saw here, as well as his experiences with other downtrodden populations in his dedication to combating social ills, inspired him to write the immortal story. (Lee, 2013)

Why is this important? It is important because literature done like Dickens, like Upton Sinclair, like John Steinbeck, and the list goes on and on is fading from the commercial eye. Meaning and social activism are being replaced by entertainment and social distraction. This shift in art is a major one. It is as if the entire publishing world is openly embracing "bread and circuses" rather than the meaning, awareness, and social activism that art has always been since its inception.

Charles Dickens and the highest-selling author in 2022, both were attempting to entertain with their stories. Art is and always has been an entertaining source. There is nothing wrong with this and it is the very fact that art is entertaining that makes it something appealing to the masses. However, I don't think any historian could look to any part of history and say that art was originally meant to be a distraction. It is only a perverse use of art that makes it a distraction in our contemporary society.

However, art and especially literature is being used as distraction each year, every year. When most or at least many of the top-selling books in any given year are solely books that distract, art becomes something other than self-expression. When millions of others are seeking to express themselves in an artistic way and cannot be or are not heard due to a system that only covets and values those who can create art that the masses want, art becomes something other than self-expression. What does it become? Distraction. It becomes another way to ensure that the people are not focusing on the well-being of society or even the well-being of themselves. It ensures that another false idol is created by the power centers of society to ensure that Juvenal's clarion call almost 2000 years ago was as true then as it is today.

In *A Christmas Carol* (2003), Charles Dickens condemns greed above all things. It is Ebenezer Scrooge's greed that molds him into the monster that treats the Cratchits and everyone else around him with such obnoxious disdain and hierarchical cruelty. Dickens published the book in 1843. Unlike escapist literature, Dickens was *presenting* an argument. These arguments are found throughout his literature and there is no book by Charles Dickens that does not make or have a social component that is asking us to re-examine or open our eyes and see the world around us in a different way. Dickens argued for us to get involved and become a part of the world around us. Today's almighty market.... which exists a mere one hundred and seventy-two years after Dickens penned that immortal work, argues for us to get distracted and forget the social ills of the world around us. This signals decay in all its forms and is endlessly tragic to the greatness that art is for our hearts, for our psyches, and for our society.

Furthermore, this distraction is being written with ever-growing frequency by artificial intelligence. There are many "AI novel writing programs" out there that will use a formula to compose a story that will tug at the heartstrings and evoke a massive amount of pathos. Computers are cheaper than authors, and these formula-driven machines are capable of making literature cheaper – and emptier – than ever before in history. Right now, they can provide plot-lines, themes, characters, and story ideas, and it does not take much speculation to see that soon they may take the place of great human authors everywhere.

It is a similar story in the music industry. Here, the music label is everything. They are the publishing company of the music world, and almost every artist is at the complete mercy of the music label. What does the music label want? Money. Money has always driven the mass production of music, and therefore, it is subject to all the same whims as the book industry. Therefore, music tends to bend to the same desires of capitalistic culture that literature does. It is molded and shaped by popularity rather than meaning. Popularity, however, becomes a godlike figure that determines worth and sets cultural norms, societal attitudes, etc. For instance, the most popular pop star in the United States today drove a 1,226% increase in traffic in 2023 to a voter registration and assistance website. This was within a single hour after the singer directed her fans to do so in a social media post (Sullivan, 2023). This is a positive form of the herd instinct because, obviously, voter registration is laudable. However, it illustrates the herd instinct when it comes to the popularity of pop stars and the music industry. This herd instinct has the potential to become and, in many ways, already is like a widespread virus that is continuing to alter, change, and, depending on your viewpoint, destroy much of the meaning created by all art forms in the previous generations.

Is this subjective? Of course. Art is subjective. Anyone could make an argument that today's literature is as meaningful as Shakespeare, or that today's pop music is as meaningful as the Rolling Stones or The Doors. The concept of meaning is a personal concept, and because it is personal, there is no clear answer to these questions. However, it seems like it would take quite a bit of intellectual maneuvering to adequately compare the immortal and very deep story of *Hamlet* to the romance novels that dominated the charts in 2022.

Similarly, it would take a very well-reasoned and strongly made argument to state that Creedence Clearwater Revival's epic protest song, "Fortunate Son" is less meaningful and impactful of a song as the current number one hit that reigned supreme on the Billboard charts, which is a young woman singing about the heartbreak and empowerment that she derived from a breakup with her celebrity boyfriend. In both cases, the concept of distraction from the major issues in current times is obvious. The almost constant theme of breakups and relationship issues serve as red herrings from the crushing poverty, the enormous inequalities in wealth, the consistent military action that is being taken, and an almost endless amount of other significant and very important issues of our current society.

There is an empirical basis that has been established for the simplification and creation of less meaningful music. Varnum et al. (2021) analyzed music in the United States over six decades, from 1958-2016. In fact, they examined over 14,500 songs in an effort to understand ecological and cultural factors that may be responsible for shifts in lyrical simplicity in songs. The researchers found that the simpler the song in our culture, the higher it reached on the charts, and, consequently, the much greater success the song garnered. This phenomenon is especially present when there was a very dominant pop song that had especially novel, or gimmicky, lyrics.

What does this correlation say for the music industry? It seems to suggest that the gatekeepers for music, just as the gatekeepers of publishing, are almost entirely concerned with what will sell, rather than what is meaningful, impactful, and culturally relevant art. Bubblegum music, with their upbeat choruses, dance-along lyrics, and melodies that you just can't get out of your head because they're so catchy, are the new Neil Youngs, Marvin Gayes, Led Zeppelins, and James Browns.

This is where the concept of algorithms comes into the picture. Algorithmic composition, or automated composition, is the process of making music with a minimal amount of human intervention (Maurer, 1999). In other words, the concept is that music is now being engineered using computers and mathematical premises to create a string of sounds that will manipulate our brains into falling in love with it. Jim Morrison had the foresight to imagine that this could come into existence all the way back in the 1960s when he noted this in an interview (Fischer, 2018). A variety of bands since the year two thousand have talked about the concept of algorithms as a way to create catchy rhythms and beats that will play to the listener's desires and create a steady stream of irresistible bubblegum pop music.

Journalist Pendlebury (2022) of CNET states that this concept is not only already amongst us, but that we are moving toward a, "wholly computer generated pop future" (para. 7) Drew Silverstein, cofounder of his own recording studio, states that this type of automation has existed for a long time already. He states that he believes that this type of automated song-making is a natural evolution in music-making technologies that is, "both amazing and scary at the same time" (para 8).

Silverstein runs his own music company, and so I can see wherein he and the large record labels believe the concept of computer animation is amazing. However, to the millions of musicians out there who pour their hearts and souls into creating both music and lyrics that are meaningful and important in the way they impact our culture and affect society, the concept of algorithms and automated music seems downright terrifying.

However, if pop culture has taught us anything, it is sadly that greed wins. It seems likely that the trend of automation in music will continue, and in continuing, it will continue to marginalize the independent artists in music. We, on the other hand, will be continually distracted by the computer-programmed and scientifically researched jingles that we have grown accustomed to since the 2000s. As long as we are distracted by catchy enough refrains and attractive enough music videos, we will likely not lament the loss of deeply meaningful social commentary and protest music that reached our hearts and changed our minds.

Art, in all its facets, can serve and has served as a beacon of light for the human race. It creates political awareness, cultural and moral corrections, and, most of the time, serves as the divining rod to point us in the right direction. Art helps us to re-examine ourselves and to question the world around us rather than just obey. This has been our history and our collective experience. Without art, it would be a much dimmer and bleaker existence that we have on this earth. Therefore, the purity of our art in all its forms is so important for the well-being of our species. It is hard to make a cogent argument against the importance of art to our existence.

However, the systems and levers that create and control art in our society are increasingly straying from the age-old formula that has been set up in the past in free societies. The gatekeepers who are able to make art available are being led astray by the desire for profit. Art is consequently becoming made to be pleasing to the masses and lucrative and nothing more. This trend has diverted our attention toward minutia and away from the bigger cultural and sociopolitical issues on which art was so accustomed to commenting.

As noted, Ezra Pound very aptly called artists the "antennae of the race." However, in our present, art is serving a role that far more aptly can be called distractor of the race. Obviously, any mode of self-expression is art, and therefore, today's art is art. However, it is art with impure influences. Any art that is manufactured and presented for public consumption has to pass very specific litmus tests based on the form of art it is and the medium for which it is being manufactured. Some level of this is inevitable. However, art as a general concept has largely lost its edge and its duty to inform the public, to create awareness, and to change minds on a wide variety of social issues. Some art still does. But it is becoming increasingly rare due to the system of gatekeepers who wield the power to permit art or not permit art that reaches the masses based on their own self-interest. The creation of art is the yardstick of culture, and the more that those who do it are forced to conform to standards that inhibit their true self-expression, the less effective art becomes. Unknowingly, and unwittingly, the art centers of society are being ransacked by the systems of society that force art to be put into a small box of popular parameters that will only be seen if it affects us in very specific, predetermined, and prepackaged ways. These parameters in which art is forced to operate are used to create works that serve as false idols to the public. We consequently begin chasing the ideals and culture that art creates based on what the gatekeepers want us to be chasing. We are left with false idols mirroring their needs rather than authentic art. These false idols that are erected for us by a wayward and motive-driven industry stunt our cultural and personal growth.

These false idols that steer the direction of the industry are hardly limited to affecting the artistic expression of every kind. They affect other types of self-expression as well, and especially the traditional self-expression that occurs on the internet and social media. Let's examine the erection of false idols on these very contemporary mediums.

Chapter 7

The Internet and Social Media

In the late 1960's, the United States Defense Department funded the development of a program called, "The Advanced Research Projects Agency Network" (ARPANET). This was essentially a way to send and receive data securely so that it could not be intercepted by any outside entities. It was an information system without a central core that could be targeted, and it linked computers to Pentagon-funded research facilities. (Featherly, 2023).

The ARPANET system was the direct forerunner to the Internet. In the late 1960s through the 1970s, the concept of ARPANET was utilized and, experimented with and tested by military, research, and academic institutions. The result was a massive collection of networks, all communicating with each other to share information. In the 1980s, the Internet was officially born. It would take until the 1990s for it to be a household term since this is when the World Wide Web was invented by Tim Berners Lee. (Featherly, 2023).

The original Internet was crude and simple. There was no Windows, and the Internet did not have nearly the amount of information or features than it does today. It gained greater and greater amounts of users for the many features it did have, but it was not until around 1993 that the Internet began to explode into a nationwide and worldwide phenomenon. This was due to the fact that 1993 marked the first web browser available to the public on a widespread basis. (National Science and Media Museum, 2020).

After 1993, the Internet gained much greater popularity. Its popularity was a force that enabled it to spread with a speed and an influence like few, if any, inventions in the history of humanity. At present, it is estimated to have at least 5.35 billion users. The average American spends a stunning 47 hours per week on the internet. (Pelchen, 2024) In other words, the average American spends more time on the Internet than it takes to do a full-time job.

At no time in all of human history have human beings had more access to information or to the ability to connect with each other more than now, due to the Internet. It has made available the ability to spread knowledge in a way never before seen or perhaps even imagined in human history. It creates fertile soil for our connection with each other and with ideas that could facilitate and enact social change on a level that is almost inconceivable.

What do we do with all that connection? How do we use all that incredible knowledge that could do so much to help us change and create a better world?

According to Petrosyan (2023), 93.3% of us use it for communicating with other people through some sort of messaging. 91.8% of us use it for sending emails. 74.6% of us use it for engaging in social media. It is worth mentioning that these are the most popular uses for the Internet. All that connection is primarily used to send messages to one another. The Internet has an enormous capacity to bring us meaningful information that can change our lives and the lives of those around us. However, our primary usage for it is to communicate with one another. This was already something we could do through phones or letters or the often-forgotten concept of walking up to each other and actually speaking to one another.

Coming in at fourth is using financial services, which compose 74.3% of the usage of the internet. Shopping ranks at 74.1%, watching videos online ranks at 70.1%, participating video calls comes in at 65.6% and the list goes on and trails out from there. (Petrosyan, 2023).

The list is revealing. It is also hard to dispute when one examines the Internet. For every one site that discusses concrete and credible information that could be utilized for any number of constructive reasons, there are a thousand sites devoted to social, gossip, and, many times, illicit and illegal material. Every click to go to websites seems connected to a flurry of advertisements seeking our attention and popping up in our vision. These advertisements use every conceivable way of communicating to our base instincts and drives us to purchase products that we don't need. However, we have come to look at them as necessary gatekeepers to the information that we so direly seek. They form the basis of how we spend our heartbeats watching, devouring, and investing our time.

I often wonder what the great Roman satirist and social critic Juvenal would think of the Internet. As he did in ancient Rome, I can imagine him finding ways to publish and create witty and interesting posts that would mock not only the powers that be in our society, but, would attack us and our willingness to be a part of a system full of so many flaws. I also wonder if his voice would be drowned out today since social media and the internet host a forum so diffuse that a single voice cannot be heard within it.

There is, of course, no way of knowing this. But what seems very clear is that he would see the Internet as another form of the Coliseum of his day. We are completely and utterly distracted by the Internet and this is especially evidenced by the concept that we spend, in one form or another, almost as many hours on it as we do at our job. In some ways, the Internet is the Mother Lode of social distraction, used to make sure that we are always occupied with the hegemony that rules our lives.

What, then, is so meaningful about these new modes of communication that have become the center of meaning and value in so many of our lives? Let's examine the values that are created by what we covet. In other words, what makes these communication systems so worth our time and breath and energy?

The first email was sent in 1971. A man named Ray Tomlinson sent it. He contributed to the development of ARPANET. As far back as the 1960s, computer users were able to send messages to different users on the same computer. However, Ray Tomlinson developed the first application for network email that enabled users to send messages to users on other computers. He did so by combining the 'SNDMSG' and 'CYPNET' programs. This allowed messages to be sent from one computer to the other for the first time. (MIT, 2024) It changed everything.

With email came a new form of communication. Email was an impersonal but convenient way to communicate with others. It all started with, "SNDMSG." Within fifty years, "SNDMSG," would transform into personal webpages, social media, and every other conceivable mode of communication that we have via the Internet today.

It is important to note that there were very few, if any, false idols, created from email. Email was almost no different than letter writing. After its invention in 1971, it became a standard of use in early computing and continued to grow until 1994. Before 1994, email was largely used to connect one person to another in a meaningful way. It was letter writing only without having to use stamps and wait long times in between replies. There were no email attractions that everyone had to be a part of or watch; there were no major celebrities or businesses hosting email parties or events in which everyone felt they had to be a part. Email was, in a Walt Whitman sort of way, a celebration of self. In other words, when we had email, we did not engage in the suicide of the self in terms of our self-expression. We retained who we are.

Then came 1994. When the very brilliant George Orwell wrote his great work *1984*, it was 1949. In many ways, one can argue that Orwell (2021) hit the right decade for the totalitarian state, but in other ways, one can argue that the book could've been called 1994. This was the moment that commercialism collided with the Internet and email became commercialized. This was the moment that spam entered into the realm of the Internet and therefore, it was the introduction and inception of the false idols in the realm of cyberspace (Gibbs, 2017). It was in April 1994 that two lawyers created what is now known as SPAM. SPAM is any kind of unwanted solicitation on the Internet that is sent out on a large scale and is almost universally used to elicit financial or other personal information from the user. When Outlook and AOL arrived in 1994, it was very clear that it would not take very long before this incredible tool to connect us, that was called email, would be used for malicious and capitalistic purposes as well.

So then, email was a constructive force that started in the intellectual halls of MIT, was made convenient and extremely accessible through Ray Tomlinson, and then was widely commercialized in the following two decades. It started as a way to connect people and form bonds and it became a way to create revenue and make advertisements. It still, however, was not a major wellspring of false idols and remains even today a tremendous tool for human beings across the planet to connect and communicate with each other in a meaningful way. It, like the Internet itself, was an incredible tool that has enabled us an immense amount of new opportunities but that was also corrupted and flawed. These new tools would soon become distorted and would turn into the proverbial gateway drugs that we use to stop our ability to focus on everything that doesn't matter and nothing that does.

Therefore, email was born in 1971. The Internet was born in 1983. Both of these entities had a widespread impact on our culture and existence. But it wasn't until 1996 that the "bread and circuses" that these new vehicles of modern culture presented went on steroids. The social media platform Six Degrees was founded by a man named Andrew Weinreich in May of 1996. Millions of people signed up for it, which hosted the first concept of social media profiles, and everyone having their own. However, the Internet did not have nearly as wide an audience in 1996 as it does today, and this made the social network extremely limited. In October, 2001, Ryze was the next social media site, and it was used for business networking. Then came Friendster in 2002. This was used as a dating site, a way to meet people without the terror and difficulty of actually having to look them in the eye and talk to them in person, and it is typically given the stature of the first social media platform. It, and its competitor, MySpace, began to revolutionize the cultural concept of meeting other people and engaging with others in a meaningful social way (Ngak, 2014).

Email and the Internet both had their flaws. Both became increasingly used by the malicious to manipulate and, draw in, and corrupt. They also became massive tools of distraction in that we were looking at them all day rather than looking at our lives and our society and what may be truly valuable to us. However, for any negativity that they contained, they also contained a great deal of good. It is hard to argue that the outburst of information and widespread connection that we felt toward one another through these entities were negative at first.

However, social media was a different entity. Social media has made the Internet extremely personal on every level. Having a webpage, for example, on the Internet in its inception was not generally something one did instead of a job. If you ask someone who was young in the 1980s and the 1990s who had a webpage what they wanted to do when they grew up, they would generally give a standard answer that was rooted in civic life, such as a lawyer, doctor, and so on. These have been the answers throughout almost all of the twentieth century. However, the views of the generation reared on social media, that is, those using the internet in the twenty-first century, had a different answer.

Most of them want to be "social media influencers" when they grow up. About 86% of young individuals, in a survey by CBS in 2019, stated they want to become a social media influencer (Min, 2019). What is an influencer? An influencer is a type of social media marketing that consists of endorsements made by entities seen as influential or are regarded as experts in a particular area.

In other words, social media influencers are people who quite often have no credentials to say anything about what they're talking about but have found a way to manipulate and sometimes coerce a large group of people. They do this to an audience who is generally emotionally thinking and not critically thinking to get them to follow them online. This following and, in most cases, blind loyalty to this person has resulted in large and small businesses, individuals, and other groups paying them to advertise their merchandise to said individuals.

Merriam-Webster's Dictionary (2024) defines a cult as, "great devotion to a person, idea, object, movement, or work" (para 2). The definition seems to fit the concept of social media influencer perfectly. Using this definition, it is safe to call social media influencers cult leaders who are indoctrinating the individuals they are able to indoctrinate. The key difference between the traditional usage of cult and this usage is that in a traditional cult, individuals are devoted to a person, idea, object, movement, or work that is greater than themselves and that they truly believe is meaningful. The cult of social media influencers depart from this definition in that they are truly devoted to a person and the companies that sell the products that the person endorses.

The concept of a cult is very important to the concept of social media. Before social media, cults were very present and their presence had all of the same elements that exist in social media now. Heaven's Gate, a cult led by Marshall Applewhite and Bonnie Nettles, was formed in 1974. The two met while they were in a psychiatric hospital and after that meeting, they renamed themselves "Bo" and "Peep" and took a 6-month long road trip across the United States. Nettles then died in 1985. However, Applewhite kept the cult together and once the Internet was widespread and accessible in the 1990s, his cult began using it. The Internet was how Heaven's Gate was able to sustain themselves financially, and, recruit new members.

In March 1997, thirty-nine members of Applewhite's cult committed suicide. The suicides were very uniform. Each person dressed in a black suit and wore sneakers. Each person ate applesauce containing barbiturates. Each person drank vodka. Then, all of the cultists covered their heads with bags and put purple shrouds over themselves. Finally, they lied down and left their carnal selves behind them as they believed they would spiritually ascend to a spacecraft which was tied to the Hale-Bopp Comet, which was passing by the earth precisely when they did this. They died with the belief that they were going to their new home in space. Applewhite was one of the thirty-nine individuals who were found dead. (Hafford, 2017).

Applewhite persuaded his believers based on his charisma and his skewed and dangerous belief systems. His ideology that one has to physically leave their human form in order to ascend to the mother ship that will carry them home is not a readily easy pill to swallow. However, using his charisma and his wife's charisma, he was able to do so. As noted, the inception of the Internet aided him after his wife died to gain followers. These followers would never have been able to connect with him if it were not for the Internet. It was a major vehicle through which he could indoctrinate others.

This cult and all those who precede it, including the Jonestown Massacre, the Manson family, NXIVM, Angel's Landing, and so on are, in some ways, the forerunner of the social media generation. Using the definition of cult above, the social media "influencer" meets every facet of the definition. Even the language on virtually any social media platform has the ring of cult vernacular. Many platforms even use the term "follower" to designate people who are fans or are interested in the other person. Every social media "influencer" must create a message or a platform that continually gains interest from the followers. While social media is not typically a place where followers engage in radical behavioral change, it is most certainly a place where behavioral change is constant based on the message of the "influencer."

There are many similarities between a traditional cult and modern-day social media. However, there is one immense and key difference. Cult leaders often incorporate death and suicide in their message of creating a better existence. Social media influencers generally have, of course, no such message. Cult leaders generally have a great vision for what is to come or how to change ourselves to become at peace or perfect or better. Social media "influencers" are also often selling a message in which one can better themselves or to make someone feel better either implicitly or explicitly. However, almost all of the indoctrination that social media engenders is economically based. There is no denying that social media "influencers" and cultists are closer to being synonyms than most people are probably willing to admit.

In other words, when one examines the psychological motives for social media influencers and cult leaders there are striking similarities. Both intrinsically are interested in promoting their own vanity. Both enjoy hearing themselves speak and getting their name and sense of self promoted and delivered into the sea of people that we call our world. Therefore, both are essentially interested in their identity and their sense of self. The cult leader and social media influencer are both egomaniacs by definition who require followers to bathe them in a sea of vanity that often hints at much deeper emotional and psychological problems.

Perhaps most interestingly, the cult leader and the social media influencer are generally both interested in benefiting economically from the followers that they have. However, the cult leader generally is not looking to climb any economic ladder or create a fortune based on their leadership. The social media influencer is doing precisely that with its corporate sponsors and its promise of an endless amount of advertising dollars. This cannot help but pervert the message of the social media influencer. The social media influencer, therefore, has an ulterior motive that the cult leader may or may not. This further perverts the message and creates even more erroneous and perverted false idols. It is an economic cult that is fronting as a spiritual or health or other cult-like entity. The fact that there is such a staunch economic motive makes it inherently false, and it serves as a barrage of messages and herds that only critical thinking can help us avoid and repair.

Therein lays the issue. The more we are brainwashed by the cult leaders we see on the Internet, on television, on social media, and elsewhere, the less we think for ourselves. The less we think for ourselves, and the more our democracy, our way of living, our identity, and our forward progression in history dies. The stakes could not be higher. As Dylan Thomas said in his immortal 1951 poem *Do Not Go Gentle into That Good Night,* we must, "Rage, rage against the dying of the light" (Thomas, 1971). In this case, the dying of the light is our very humanity, our sense of self, and our identity. We are fighting against who the system wants us to be.

Who gets to be at the top of this cult that is social media? Who gets to indoctrinate us on a daily basis and infiltrate many facets of our lives by leading us with the power of the herd behind them? Who are these so-called mortal gods we have elevated to god-like status in our consciousness and in our society? Let's examine these modern-day Icarus-like figures of idolatry.

According to Cuello-Garcia et al. (2020) of the Journal of Clinical Epidemiology, there were more than 3.8 billion individuals utilizing social media around the world in 2020. It is safe to assume that that number has only grown as the pandemic raged on and social networks were constrained. Many estimates discuss a number significantly higher and it is very likely that a significant majority of the individuals in our world are utilizing social media.

The numbers are simply astounding. Facebook continues to sit atop the social media world, with more than 2.963 billion people using it (Meta Investor Relations, 2021). YouTube sits as the runner-up with 2.56 billion users (Kemp, 2021). Instagram has more than two billion (Rodriguez, 2021). TikTok has over 1.53 billion (Bursztynsky, 2021). It is important to keep in mind that during the same time period, the United Nations estimated our world population as exceeding eight billion in November 2022. This means that it is undeniable that many and probably most of our world, are mesmerized and enamored with social media. This is also what makes social media the largest and most wide-reaching marketplace for capitalistic endeavors of any and all kinds. What does the world clamor to see? What pleases the world most in terms of its digital entertainment?

Let's examine Instagram first, as it has been a growing favorite social media platform for billions. Of the top five individuals who have the most "followers," that is to say, the biggest cult, two of them are professional athletes (Forbes India, 2024). The top two have over one billion followers combined, or roughly one out of every eight people on this earth seeks to be their pseudo 'friend.' What did they do that is so worthy of being followed? By the staggering numbers, one would think they would have powers to cure the sick or to heal the masses. But no, that's not it. They are able to kick a round ball into a rectangular net. They understand formations and defenses and are excellent athletes who never stopped playing a game that many of us started playing when we were 4 or 5 years old. It is undeniable that they are tremendous athletes but to garner the respect, admiration, and "following" of a very significant percentage of the human race is astounding. These men are more false idols that we have created. They garner a seemingly endless amount of attention and adoration from every angle. However, they do not produce or create anything that benefits humanity in a meaningful way other than the thrill we get from watching them kick a ball into a goal. Besides their dribbling and their goals and the small thrill that they create in us in around fifty matches per year, we are often left with a void and hollowness in valuing them. This hollowness is filled by commercialism propelled by our vanity, that is, our desire to be like them, to be closer to them. Their images have been created like deities, and that deity is a false god of allusions and financial blessings. Again, this is all because they can kick a round ball into a rectangular net better than other men who never decided to quit the game they started when they were 4 or 5 years old.

The third, fourth, and fifth individuals who have their following on Instagram are all in the second category (Forbes India, 2024). Each is an entertainer. These three have well over a billion followers combined. Do they perform miracles to receive such admiration from the masses? Nope. One is a widely celebrated entertainer whose greatest skills include raising his right eyebrow while the left stays without moving, acting like he's hurting people in a ring even though it is all choreographed and fake, and making blockbuster movies that no one will remember within a decade or two. He is ranked behind a singer and actress who rose to prominence as a child by acting in a show for children. She used that platform to generate a series of other acting gigs and then eventually launched a music career. Honorably, she has engaged in a great deal of philanthropy with her success. This is, perhaps, the most worthy aspect of her to be followed. However, she has created and packaged herself in such a way that inspires millions of others to come close to worshiping her. The last false idol in the top five is one who can be starkly contrasted with the other two entertainers on Instagram's top following. She can probably best be described as a "personality." Although we all have a personality, her personality was instantly elevated to worldwide acclaim due to the fact that her parents, her half-sisters, and her half-brothers, were all well-known people. In other words, she was coronated as worthy of all this attention because she was born into it in the same way the caste system of India or the feudal system of old created status by birth.

These are the top five most influential social networkers' on the face of the planet... at least according to Instagram. Cumulatively, something in the vicinity of 25% of the human race is tuned into those five people. None of those five people produce any substantial product and are no more worthy than anyone else to deserve the vast majority of people who are enamored by them. None of them do any perceivable thing that directly makes the world a substantially better place, with the sole exception of charitable money given. However, we as a group spend, in many cases, more time staring at them and examining their existences than looking at our own in a way that could cultivate and bring meaningful change to it.

Let's examine another social media behemoth and the further creation of "bread and circuses" that occupy our mind and distract our thoughts. Facebook, as described above, remains the number one most-used social media outlet since its inception in 2004. The number two followed entity on Facebook, at the time of this writing is a multinational company from South Korea (Forbes India, 2024). The company creates products that have taken over much of the American market. In other words, the number two entity that is followed on Facebook is a multinational corporation. What lifesaving technology does it create? Cell phones. Over one quarter of the world is eagerly locked into following a for-profit behemoth who has a less-than-stellar record in regard to financial practices. For example, the BBC reported in December

2019 that Chairman Lee Sang-hoon was jailed for union sabotage (BBC News, 2019). This man, as well as twenty-five other employees engaged in countless efforts to undermine attempts for the workers of this nightmarish company to engage in any union activity. They have also been formally accused, by their own country and government, of a number of labor rights violations, including health and safety concerns for the workers, very low wages, worker deaths, exploitation, and, as noted above, the favorite of multinational corporations everywhere, union busting. It has been accused and charged for abusing child labor issues in its factories all over the world. This company is the number two followed entity on the single largest social media platform in the world. This is who we choose to admire. This is the face of our modern day cult leader.

The next false god is a familiar one. It is the great and mighty soccer player we have touched on already. Because it wasn't enough for him to have billions of users and other social media outlets, he has millions more on Facebook. As with his exalted status on Instagram, he is one of the most followed people on Facebook (Business Connect India, 2023). Remember, he just kicks a round ball into a rectangular net.

The next most popularly followed entity on Facebook is not a person and not a corporation. It is a show. It is a show that is a comedy and serves the sole purpose of escapism to those who watch it. Escapism is the act of watching something to distract oneself from the world around us. It is distraction. Comedy is distraction. It features a childlike adult who is navigating in an adult world. It takes us away from reality in the same way that any romance novel does. One hundred and sixty-three million of us are locked into a cult-like following of this comedy. (Business Connect India, 2023).

It must also be noted that it is wrought with 'clickbait.' Clickbait is essentially any advertisement or image that is used to take our attention away from whatever we are viewing. Clickbait is designed for the sole purpose of creating more money. It is in the form of advertisements. Therefore, while you are engaging in whatever your passion is, you are often and endlessly torpedoed with distracting imagery geared toward stealing your time and creating revenue for the channel. This is the only form of distraction that in any way mars this concept.

The next most worshipped entity on Facebook is a television station (Business Connect India, 2023). That television station belongs to one of the major governments in the world. It is state media and, therefore, is totally controlled by the state. It has been characterized as propaganda and total disinformation by other credible television stations and credible news media outlets and watchdogs. In other words, this state-run propaganda channel indoctrinates its viewers with whatever view it says is the right one. It has no checks or balances on it and is the fifth most followed entity on the largest social media outlet in the entire world.

Lastly, another widely followed person on Facebook is a woman who is an internationally acclaimed singer (Business Connect India, 2023). She sings songs and her dancing is widely renowned. She sings and she dances and the masses stand in awe. She, like the other female singer on the list, has created a foundation to help impoverished children. However, she is no deity and she has no special powers other than to sing and to dance.

One multinational corporation. One TV show. One singer. One soccer player. Oh, and one propaganda outlet for a corrupt government. This is what we value and cherish and this is evident by how much of our time is spent on it. Every one of these entities, outside of the crafts, is a total distraction from the cultivation of ourselves or to the education that would be needed to change the world around us. Sports and celebrities continue to consume our time because they have become what we value. What we value becomes the rock upon which the commercialism that devours us is built. The erection of all social media outlets and the Internet has become a way to keep us plugged in for celebrities, sports, and entertainment in all of its forms so that we are never focusing on ourselves or our democracy for the betterment of our society.

To illustrate this using one more platform, let's examine YouTube. YouTube functions on a different engine than social networking and, at first glance, seems to be less prone to the idolatry that social media contains. YouTube has billions of users and is as large and influential a vehicle to deliver messages as they come in the Internet and social media age.

One of the most subscribed to channels on YouTube is a record label (Forbes India, 2024). It creates a variety of music that primarily centers on Indi-pop. It has reached massive appeal for presenting music and that music serves as a distraction for millions of people. That distraction likely carries those people away from a life with which they are wholly dissatisfied. The channel carries an immense amount of influence due to the adoration of the pop hits that they cultivate. It has an incredible 258 million subscribers.... 258 million people eagerly awaiting the new release of a song or a trailer. It is an Indian-based record label and this clearly indicates that India and its 1.4 billion people, according to the United States Census Bureau (2024), lusts after and is enamored with the false gods of celebrities on a level that is not unlike the United States.

Another widely subscribed to channel on YouTube is an anomaly. It is a British-created and American-run 3D animation video channel. The pretty animations feature nursery rhymes and children's songs. The videos generally have children, adults, and other humans who interact with each other in daily life. They began in 2018 and have risen to one of the most subscribed to channels at the time this is being written, and, have spent a good deal of time being immensely popular.

This 3D animation video channel contains virtually none of the concepts on which this book is based. The channel delivers content that distracts our children, and mostly very young children, but not us, from the reality around us. It delivers a service that can clearly be argued to better our lives and it obviously has a commercial element but it seems to more dominantly be a symbiotic relationship between the viewer and the content creator. It is devoid of vanity, greed, megalomania, or virtually any of the basic hooks that virtually every other social media and video platform utilizes and runs on. This concept is the model for what these incredible services and concepts that human beings have created since creating the Internet in the 1960s could be. It works on a different engine than everything else. Internet-based content can both give parents an accessible tool to utilize to either entertain or educate the children while simultaneously giving them a break to get many of the things they may have to get done, done. It boasts 171 million subscribers (Forbes India, 2024), a far cry from the Indi-pop channel noted above.

After that brief respite, we get back into the endless distraction of entertainment with another top-five most popular channel, which is an Indian-based pay television channel. Its origins are rooted in reality television, and it currently boasts six shows that garner the devotion and interest and adoration of at least 168 million subscribers. (Forbes India, 2024).

The next channel is another YouTube behemoth that reaches an immense amount of people. This channel boasts 236 million subscribers and undoubtedly many, many other viewers in addition to those subscribers (Forbes India, 2024). This channel is not a business or corporation but rather a single human being. What is he doing to gain the immense admiration of a population that is more than half of that of the United States of America? He started his YouTube career by counting to one hundred thousand on camera. This great feat, which lasted beyond twenty-four hours but was edited for the camera to be contained within twenty-four hours, was something that went 'viral.' The individual has been delivering videos ever since that emulate the masochism and absurdity that others such as Eval Knievel and *Jackass* have done from at least 1966 to present. The videos include such classics as, "I paid an assassin to try to kill me," to "I survived the plane crash." Each video drips with a clear and massive desire for the person to garner attention in any way possible. In fact, there is no message other than the subtext that people will pay attention to you if you put yourself in situations that are universally dreaded and feared. Of course, the YouTube channel that he has comes along with what is likely an endless amount of advertising dollars.

Another massively subscribed to channel on YouTube is by a Swedish video gamer. He began posting videos using specific technology that allows him to show the video game that he is playing as he talks. In other words, he plays the video game and talks as he plays and we listen to him talk as we watch him play the video game. That's it. This is how this person gained, to date, 111 million subscribers to his YouTube channel (Forbes India, 2024). Since then, he has created a wealth of other content to entertain the masses, including classics such as, "I took my car off-road... oops." This is all of what his channel does and his channel creates what is likely obscene revenue as well as garners the interest and oftentimes adoration of an almost endless amount of subscribers.

We have seen just a few of the "bread and circuses" that keep us entertained and turn our heads away from what matters and toward what provides short-term relief but long-term pain. This social media, these channels, and this entertainment serve as a drug that keeps us addicted and complacent so that we are not paying attention to or fixing the problem. Without the problem, we would not utilize the drug. But it is within the best interest of the entities that profit from our ingestion of the drug to continue to deliver it. This is how the "bread and circuses" I am describing, and not religion, become the true 'opium of the people.'

This opiate can come to dominate reality for many. In his book, *Less than Nothing: Hegel and the Shadow of Dialectical Materialism*, philosopher Slavoj Žižek states, "Beyond the fiction of reality, there is the reality of fiction" (Žižek, 2012, p.4). This general concept is certainly applicable to false idols and the many diversions they create in our lives. Much of the reality we are presented in modern-day society has elements of fiction. Both social media and celebrity are saturated with unattainable archetypes of beauty, personality, behavior, and virtually every perceived and often manufactured 'desirable' trait that the masses come to want. However, if we look closely, we can see the reality behind the fiction. The reality of the fiction is that these archetypes are false idols and often succeed in indoctrinating and leading us away from our true selves and desires.

This indoctrination in the age of the Internet causes many casualties. The amount of destruction is legion and is far too much and too comprehensive to describe in this book. However, one of them presents a terror that looms so large that it cannot be ignored. This is because it puts kindling on the fire of our ignorance, distraction, and lack of motivation to do anything to create a better existence for ourselves.

Merriam-Webster's Dictionary (2023) defines the Information Age as, "the modern age regarded as a time in which information has become a commodity that is quickly and widely disseminated and easily available especially for the use of computer technology" (para 1). The years and the moments upon which this conception began are debated. However, no one can doubt that the invention of the Internet had a major role in the Information Age.

This information, on its surface, seems incredibly wonderful. It made the widespread use of information available to everyone. It is, perhaps, only surpassed by the invention of the printing press by Gutenberg in 1440, when individuals were able to have newspapers and books on a widespread basis.

There are many key differences between these two bursts of information on a widespread scale. Books have always been perceived as credible because they are filtered by publishing companies, editors, and many other individuals who oversee a book before it is released to the public. The Internet, conversely, has no such claim. Anyone can have a website, and that website does not have to meet anything but a base standard of acceptability. There is no one who is prohibited from having a social media account or many social media accounts on which they can say anything they want within certain guidelines. Most of these guidelines involve obscenity and lewd comments both on webpages and social media accounts. None of them have the high standards that any publisher would have for any book that they put out for public consumption. Therefore, the second Information Age, the current era, is very unlike the first in 1440. Because this information has no standards; it meets no standards. In other words, there is virtually no framework for credibility for anything that is produced on the Internet, very much unlike that produced in books.

Herein lays the virus of misinformation. Misinformation is as damaging as anything to our culture, and it proves to be both a form of bread and circus and a false god that damages us as a society in a way that few other things can. Misinformation is dangerous in the same way that a lie is dangerous. Why? Because misinformation is a lie, and therefore, it has all of the destructive and horrific capabilities that any lie has ever had.

Let's examine one very recent and very horrific way misinformation impacted us. It was on January 20, 2020 that the first case of the coronavirus was recorded in the United States. By January 24, 2020 the cases in the United States had spread to two, and it became clear that COVID was a reality within the United States. By April 3rd, 2020 the CDC announced new mask-wearing guidelines for individuals to wear masks whenever they are outside of the home. On April 10th, 2020, New York State had a confirmed 159,937 cases. By May 28, 2020 the death toll from the coronavirus in the United States surpassed 100,000 people. President Trump continued to fail to wear a mask, against CDC guidelines, and encouraged businesses to stay open. This was the inception of the misinformation that was to come. (Nelson et al., 2020).

A single authority figure, the President of the United States, actively suggested that it was safe for the country to be open and that testing and any other means of protection from the virus was optional. This authority gave license to and spawned the misinformation campaign that, along with the President's words and actions, would result in countless deaths. As the CDC states, "the public is bombarded with information from often unreliable sources. Misinformation is a powerfully destructive force in this era of global communication, when one false idea can spread instantly to many vulnerable ears" (Nelson et al., 2020, para. 1).

The false ideas about COVID spread to many, many vulnerable ears. Talk shows on the ideological right, both mainstream and fringe, began spitting out conspiracy theories and lies and belief systems that misled the American public. The use of social media fanned the flames of these fires and there were factions in every crevice and facet of every social media network posting every possible falsehood about the pandemic and this virus. On the one hand, there were the all-powerful businesses. They told us to keep coming to work and to not forget the importance of what they perceive as the almighty dollar. They implicitly and sometimes explicitly urged us to dismiss the mortality risks. On the other hand, far-right groups and, especially white supremacy groups, utilized the President's words to spread their bigotry and lies on social media. There was a widespread movement to recruit followers of their misled and inane white supremacist beliefs. (Klepper & Hinnant, 2021).

As PBS reported in 2021, "this tactic has been successful: nine of the ten most viewed posts in the sample examined by researchers contained misleading claims about the safety of vaccines for the pharmaceutical companies manufacturing them. One Telegram [social media] channel saw its total subscribers jump tenfold after it leaned into COVID-19 related conspiracies" (Klepper & Hinnant, 2021, para. 4).

It was on December 11, 2020 that the first COVID vaccine was released. However, in the United States, there was such an air of skepticism and misinformation that only 2.8 million people received it by the end of December. Think about that for a moment. There is a worldwide pandemic occurring, killing people in record numbers and has likely even affected or killed someone you know. The solution is presented in a miraculously short amount of time, and it is available to you, your family, and everyone you know. The expectations of the CDC were that at least 20 million people would get the vaccine by the end of December (Spalding and O'Donnell, 2020). Given the sheer panic and terror of the situation, this seemed like a rather conservative figure. At that time, there were well over 320 million people in the country, and well over 200 million were over 18 years old. However, a mere 2.8 million got the vaccine.

By September 2020, the misinformation that was propagated by President Trump, by social media, and by the right-wing media had taken a tremendous toll. In a JMIR study examining the misinformation that was being propagated regarding the coronavirus stated that, "the use of the Internet has a risk to public health, and, in cases like this, the governments should be developing strategies to regulate health information on the Internet without censoring the population" (Cuan-Baltazar et al., 2020). They went on to state that by February 2020, months after the virus was discovered, there was virtually no academic information about the virus online that had any quality content.

Another peer-reviewed article by Van Der Linden, Roozenbeek, and Compton (2020) discussed the many fake "cures" that were propagated by social media. Some of the more popular ones noted were gargling with salt water and injecting oneself with bleach. It is crucial to note that the concept of injecting oneself with bleach came directly from someone who is seen as an authority and trustful source – again, the President of the United States. They go on to discuss videos that have been circulated through the Internet suggesting that wearing a mask actually "activates" the coronavirus. Political leaders, including the U.S. President at the time, suggested other remedies, such as hydroxychloroquine. They even note how a survey found that 28% of Americans and 50% of Fox News viewers believed that Bill Gates was going to use the COVID-19 vaccine to implement microchips in people. They also demonstrate that over 25% of the videos on YouTube about the coronavirus that were the most-watched contained lies. These lies, at the time of the study, reached over 62 million people worldwide. (Van Der Linden et al., 2020).

It is obvious that misinformation is incredibly dangerous, to say the least. It is a virus that infects our minds and damages our thought processes. Misinformation steals our greatest asset – our intelligence. It makes lemmings of many of us and coaxes us to choose the herd instinct rather than critical thought. This herd instinct forges us into non-thinking people who will, quite literally, run off a cliff. It is extremely evident when it comes to the coronavirus, especially in the United States. There were three primary movers who created the death and destruction that was needless in terms of how widespread the coronavirus became. First, there was the President who doubted its existence and promoted the welfare of business and industry rather than the welfare of his constituents. Second, there was the right-wing media empire that is willing to do whatever it takes to push the agenda of the power structure it favors. Third, there was the advent of the Internet and the interconnected ability of human beings to influence human beings through the concept of the herd. This three-headed monster could turn up into down, left into right, and right into wrong. Here we saw, very recently, the endless power and manipulation that misinformation can create. This is not new. It is likely as old as human beings. It will not end until we make it end. It existed in the concentration camps of Nazi Germany, it existed in the gulags of Russia, it exists in Putin's fake media system in contemporary Russia, and it has existed in every totalitarian regime since the beginning of time. However, we have more tools than ever to fight back and create a better existence: our own existence.

At the time that this is being written, COVID is not gone in the United States. The statistics, at the time of this writing, illustrate the herd instinct and the dangers of social media and the utter abandonment and disdain for critical thinking. According to Worldometer.com (2023), the United States has had 103,802,702 confirmed cases of the coronavirus. To put this in perspective, India, which has the next highest tally, has had 44,690,738. However, please keep in mind that India is about four times the U.S. population. The United States saw 1,123,836 of our brothers and sisters die from the coronavirus. The next highest mortality count is Brazil, with 699,276. If misinformation did not exist, that is, if we valued something else other than the herd and found meaning in more things than emulating each other, who can say how many more of us may be alive? Who can say how many people would still have their loved ones in their lives and at their dinner tables if this misinformation was stopped? The dark side of social media and the Internet has never looked darker. How many other ways have social media and the Internet, in all its forms, distorted who we are and enabled us to walk down that dark path?

If we retained our identity, perhaps these pitfalls could be avoided. Rather than the Internet being used as the great unifying force that it can be, it has been just another way for us to forget who we are and what we want for our lives.

Let's examine the history that supports this idea. In the 1990s, the Internet was made widely available to the public. The Internet at that point in time looked nothing like the Internet today. Bright and colorful webpages surfaced all over the web through simple means of webpage construction and editing. This construction and editing was made easy and available for all people to do, not through a $500 or more professional webpage building company, but by ourselves in our own homes, often using free software. Therefore, many people had their own webpage and that webpage generally consisted of a series of images and text expressing themselves in a way that is meaningful to them. Of course, businesses and companies also had websites, and on those websites, they advertised and tried to sell their products. Then, in addition to the World Wide Web, which was a way to refer to the Internet in those days, there were burgeoning Internet service providers everywhere. These service providers functioned as the toll that we had to pay in order to access the Internet. They typically came with services such as email. Therefore, the Internet service provider gave us the email and the vehicle by which we could drive onto the information superhighway that is the Internet.

Put simply, the Internet service provider forced users to pay to use the Internet and give us a server that could be used for email. Once users were on the Internet, they attained the freedom to download software that enabled them to build real estate of their own on the Internet, called the webpage. The webpage was generally used as a mode of self-expression not unlike our social media page today. However, webpages were often less concerned with what one did today or some other advertisements of self rather than about something that a person was passionate about, such as a sports team or a band. There was obviously a very personal touch, but there was very often less of an emphasis on the personal and more of an emphasis on some universally cared about bond or issue.

In other words, the Internet started as information and connection. It connected my computer to your computer and your computer to everyone else's computer. Most of us had a stake of land in this new frontier that had not been seen since the Louisiana Purchase. Our land was our webpage and our webpage was formed in a way to help us connect with other people with common interests. We also had email and direct chat and we were learning to connect with each other in a way that we had never done before. It was new and inviting and constructive. This is not to suggest that there were not many, many negative influences in so many aspects of the Internet even when it started. Wherever there are people, there will be both malice and goodness. The Internet was no exception from the start. However, the Internet was different in a very positive way during this time period, and there was something very good and almost wholesome about it.

Then came 1994. This year brought the first clickable advertisement to the Internet (Bourne, 2020). Before advertising, the Internet was a way to connect with and bond with one another. After advertising, the Internet changed. It became a capitalistic vessel for marketing products. All of a sudden, on our webpages, we had to make a choice. We could either get the paid version, which was a monthly payment that was previously foreign, or we could allow the web host to put a variety of ads on our website so that we could continue using it for free. For many, it felt invasive and that it cheapened our experience. All of a sudden, an individual who was promoting his favorite team with a website that he meticulously kept up for the public had to have a big, fat ad right in the middle of it advertising tires for a national tire company. It just didn't sit right.

After 1994, ads spread like wildfire across the Internet. Chat rooms had ads somewhere on the screen that constantly reminded the users of the corporate sponsor of their chats. Many email programs contained ads in the corner that let us know that our emailing experiences were only made possible by the good people at some clothing or other type of corporation. What started as connection and information began to look like everything else in our lives: quid pro quo. The iron law of 'this for that' began to rise up and take its dominion on the Internet just as it had already done in every other facet of our existence.

The rest of the story is well-known. In the late 90s, social media began to replace webpages as the primary source of personal expression to promote a form of what Kierkegaard or Sartre called, "authenticity" (Somogy & Guignon, 2024, para. 3). In this way, the Internet was the greatest vehicle for creating authenticity but commercialism quickly capitalized and drove authenticity off a cliff and into the ravine of conformity. The Internet should have brought us the age of the *individual*. Instead, it was twisted into becoming the age of *false idols*. The images and advertisements that were flashed on the Internet, in chat rooms, on email, and in so many other places were far more prevalent and effective at catching our eyes than traditional advertisements ever were. Why? We saw them more. We spent many more hours on the Internet and using instant messages, chat rooms, text messages, emails, and the endless means of communication than we ever spent watching television.

Once again, it becomes very evident that the concept of the herd instinct or herd morality is amongst the single greatest enemies of humanity in every conceivable way. This herd instinct is dominant and prevalent in regard to the Internet. In fact, the Internet is largely *based* on the concept of herd instinct. Advertisers pay to put their ads throughout every aspect of our Internet, social media, and our world. The Internet has become an antagonist in regard to individuality because of advertising and the herd instinct that it creates. To be fair, it is not only advertising. It is any mass migration or motion of people in any direction. The Internet, and especially social media, facilitate our tendency to move and behave in a herd or to follow the crowd in a way that nothing ever has and probably ever will in the history of human society. It is amongst the most preeminent forms of "bread and circuses" that our species have ever known. It keeps us distracted and we continue to lose sight of our values and what we may actually deem truly important for our lives. It started in the 1990s and accelerated in a way that has been like nothing else after the year 2000. The Information Age, in all of its greatness and glory, quickly became The Misinformation Age came when we seemed to stop thinking for ourselves and trumpeting our own values. Instead, we became complicit in following the leader after becoming distracted by all of the pretty commercial colors being flashed before our eyes endlessly and in every direction. Due to all the misinformation and all of the bias, there are few, if any, universally recognized 'true' or 'credible' sources. From encyclopedias to dictionaries to reputable academic sources, everything is now being improperly regarded as biased. The Internet was the turning point and 1994 became the moment when everything changed.

The future of how the Internet will be shaped remains in question. The aggressive stance of the Trump Administration against Huawei or the legislation passed in Congress to prospectively ban TikTok illustrates the battle for commercial and political control rages on over the Internet. This battle for power and control will undoubtedly continue to contribute to the direction and manifestation of false idols in cyberspace.

Chapter 8

Video Games

A young child walks into therapy one day. He has short, dark hair and very innocent and happy blue eyes. When you look at him, you can see there is not an ounce of malice in his heart or dishonesty in his face. He comes in and sits down in a seat across from the therapist. He is 11 years old. His name is Noah.

"How are you doing Noah?" The therapist asks. They sit in a warm and comfortable room. There is sunlight coming in the window to the side of the therapist and Noah. It provides gentle warmth and gentle light to the session.

"Good."

"What have you done since our last session?"

"Nothing," he says shyly.

"Nothing? For the whole week?" The therapist asked incredulously. "That's a long time of doing nothing," he says and he smiles.

"Well, no. I mostly played video games."

"Video games? That's what you said last week!"

"Yeah, they're a big part of my life."

"Will you tell me about them?"

Noah's eyes become filled with excitement. "Of course."

"Well tell me about your favorite game. I want to know about what occupies most of your time when you play video games. Tell me what the premise is of the game you like most."

Noah does not pause very long before he begins to reply.

"In this game, I get to pick my character. Then I have to choose between game modes, which can be creative mode or survival mode. There are other game modes but those are the basic two…"

"What's the difference?"

"Well, in creative mode you just continue to accrue resources and you can't take any damage, meaning you can't get hurt at all or die or anything like that. And you have all the resources available to you. In survival mode, you spend your time gathering resources and you have a bunch of monsters come and do whatever they can to try to take what you have and hurt your character."

"They sound like they are very opposite modes to one another. But both modes sound like they're based on resources. In creative mode, it sounds like since you have all of the resources you can just create the world you want to create. In survival mode, it sounds like you're creating a world and then protecting it from the outside world. What is the point of the game?"

"The point is to build worlds with a bunch of different resources that you mine for and to build the world you want to build. You get the full power to build the entire world based on those resources and the world just goes on and on and on."

"Do you like building your own world?"

"I love it. I love everything about the game."

"Why do you think you like building your own world, Noah? Do you feel like you're escaping the one you are already in?"

"Yeah, I guess you could say that. I just love the game."

"Okay, so you've built your world with the resources you have. What does that look like?"

"I build castles and houses and boats and farms and tree houses and gardens and bridges and cities and everything."

"It sounds like you built a pretty great place."

"Yeah, it is pretty great."

"It sounds pretty fun, too."

"Yeah, it is. There are three worlds in it and you can build in all of the worlds and in the end you could beat the Dragon and exit all of the worlds. The Dragon is in the underworld and that's the bad place. I've beat him thirty-seven times now. Since all that, I just like playing the game and building in the overworld."

"How much time do you spend playing this game?" The therapist asks as he writes a note in his notebook.

"Most of the day."

"Most of the day?"

"If is not a school day, I eat my breakfast, and I play the entire day until I go to bed."

"It never gets old?"

"Nope."

This is a very common session format between the therapist who works with children. The next steps will often involve understanding what the game means to the child, why he is utilizing it to occupy almost all of his conscious existence that is not school (if he is using it to escape), and so on. However, one thing is undeniable: Noah spends almost all of his time playing this game.

According to a survey done by C.S. Mott Children's Hospital (2020), nine out of ten parents state that their child plays too many video games. According to the same poll, 54% of parents report that their teenager plays three or more hours a day of video games. Three or more hours a day is a remarkable amount of time and this time consumes a significant portion of any child's day in any child's life.

Let's look at the game that Noah was dedicating much of his life to playing. He said that the game was built on the concept of building a world based on resources. Does this sound familiar? The storyline in the game borrows from the materialistic and capitalistic notion that one must gain resources for themselves and build their own world with them. This is fundamentally mirroring the basic life of any of us today. The message and the indoctrination become clear: the world is full of resources and you must pillage and cultivate a means by which you can attain those resources because this is the purpose of life. Did you notice how there was no actual purpose to the game but to gain resources and build with those resources?

There are two basic modes. The first, survival mode, pits you against the world. In other words, the child playing this game has to fend off a wide array of enemies, in the form of different beings, to retain his or her resources and fulfill what appears to be their purpose in the game. In creative mode, you are not against the world. You are free to gain and cultivate all of the resources you want to build the best and most extravagant world as you can.

This concept cannot help but mirror our lives again. For the vast bulk of us who are not wealthy, life becomes survival mode. We are pitted against each other to compete in a capitalist system that is based on competition. This is the equivalent of entering the workforce and using your resources to take and get whatever you need so that you can go home and build your house with your family and your resources. The concept of creative mode is different. There, you are simulating what it is to have extreme wealth. There is no competition for resources because you have so many, and with those resources, you can build a world wherein there is no limit to how much you can have or what you can do with all that you have. It is the apex of having endless material resources.

Therefore, the creation of false idols begins to become very clear in the gameplay alone. No child is consciously thinking about the messages portrayed but when one steps back and examines them, they mirror our capitalist system and our economic beliefs are revealed. The value system here is one of ownership and wealth. The concept of materialism lies at the core of the video game concepts and themes, and wealth and poverty, competition and excess are heavily pushed both unconsciously and consciously into the gamer's mind as he plays.

All video games have a storyline. All of the storylines are written by individuals with an interest in the player buying more video games. Therefore, in this syllogism, many video games are written using themes that indoctrinate or create a belief system in the player of that video game that encourages the buying of more video games. Who can deny that every first-person shooter game, which compose the great bulk of the best-selling video games, are actively encouraging the use of guns and gun violence to achieve goals and create resolution to problems? The very premise of every one of those games hinges on the concept that the gun is the way to solve the problem. In other words, physical violence is being presented eternally in video games as a way to remedy a conflict.

In an article by Granic et al. (2014), the authors write that in the United States alone, 91% of children between the ages of 2 years old to 17 years old play video games. Ninety-one percent. They go on to note that a nationally conducted representative study found that up to 99% of boys and 94% of girls play video games. There are certainly exceptions, and it is important not to marginalize those exceptions, but it is almost safe to say that pretty much every child in the United States of America plays video games at one time or another. When that statistic is juxtaposed with the fact that the majority of those children are playing them more than three hours per day, it becomes clear that video games are an incredibly powerful force in influencing our children, and therefore, our society. To put this in context, according to *Forbes*, the gaming industry is worth more than the music and movie industries combined. In 2022, the global gaming industry grossed $184.4 billion whereas the global music industry generated $26.2 billion and the global movie industry generated $26 billion in box office revenue (Aurora, 2023). Examining and understanding the messages behind video games and how they are affecting the thought process of children like Noah seems imperative if we are to permit them the freedom to think for themselves and to escape the creation of false idols they did not want and value systems that they did not choose.

Let's begin to examine the major themes that video games create and what value systems and belief systems they cultivate in the video game player. It should be noted at the start that virtually all video games have to have an antagonist and protagonist. By this, I mean that whether it is a sports game, first-person shooter, role-playing games, etc., video games function on the premise that there must be a main character and something that opposes that main character.

We have already examined one of the highest-selling video games today by sales in the therapy session mentioned above. That game also boasts of being in the top five most-played video games of all time, according to Game Industry News (2023). As noted, it mimics and cultivates many of the more negative belief systems and ideologies in our society. It is currently affecting more minds than almost any other form of media, and almost certainly more than any scholastic material. It is entertainment that preaches ideology. The ideology it preaches is essentially survival of the fittest, or, materialistic greed. Somewhere in the vicinity of at least 750 million people, most of whom are presumably young kids, are enraptured by this video game and, on some level, whether conscious or unconscious, are being indoctrinated by its ideology.

Another one of the highest-selling games of all time boasts over a billion players, according to Game Industry News (2023). There are only about eight billion people on the earth and at least one billion of them are playing this game. What is the premise? The game player assumes the role of a mercenary. For whom does he serve as a mercenary? Of course, it is for one of the two major global corporations that he or she will offer his or her life. The game player signs up for one of these major money-making entities and fights as its mercenary. A mercenary, if you are not familiar, is defined by Merriam-Webster's Dictionary (2024) as, "one that serves merely for wages" (para. 1). If the same term is utilized as an adjective, the dictionary calls it, "serving merely for pay or sordid advantage" (para. 3). What does it list as a synonym for the term mercenary? Greedy.

So the premise of one of the highest-selling games of all time posits our character as a greedy, fight-for-yourself entity who partners with a dominant and worldwide corporation to kill others, to defuse bombs, and to engage in a wealth of other self-serving paths requiring one person to destroy or diminish another person in some way. This is, of course, all in the name of glory for the 'almighty' corporation and symbiotically for self-gratification and personal glory.

It is not hard to see the ideology beginning to erupt again. This is hegemony and it has been omnipresent throughout this discourse on video games as well as in every chapter in this book. If you were a child playing this game for, say, three to eight hours per day, I wonder what unconscious and conscious messages you would be ingesting. As noted, over one billion people are doing just that. This game has been a major force in the gaming industry since its inception and shows no signs of letting up.

What's another one of the greatest and most enticing video game plots that brought many millions of users to play? It provides more of the same. It is, like the others I have mentioned, a worldwide phenomenon. Its premise? A bunch of players parachute to an island. On this island, they scavenge to find weapons and other equipment. What is the purpose? To kill the other people on the island without getting killed themselves. The place on the map where you can be safe decreases over time, forcing you to compete with the other people on the island so that you can destroy them and claim more resources on the island.

When William Golding wrote, *Lord of the Flies* (1954), he was writing a book that explored the negative side of humanity. The book was an allegory for humanity and it suggested that we would find ways to destroy each other. In many ways, it can be interpreted as a clarion call to the human race to stop engaging in endless division and hatred of one another. Golding served in World War II and what he saw profoundly affected him. He became cynical of human beings and that cynicism is strongly conveyed in the book. (Phillips, 2002).

It is hard for anyone to argue that Golding was doing anything but holding up a mirror to ourselves so that we can see the worst aspects of ourselves. The video game that is the "greatest" and most played of all time doesn't seem to be holding up a mirror and asking us to look. Instead, it seems to be holding out an invitation and asking us to enjoy our annihilation. In other words, it exploits the worst aspects of us. What can a child possibly take from a game like this?

First and foremost, it suggests that we are alone in the world and that we have to protect ourselves. It suggests that material resources, which can, in virtually every game, be a metaphor for currency or economics, are of the utmost importance and are imperative to the meaning of life. It suggests that our fellow human being is our antagonist and that in the quest for resources, we must destroy the obstacle of others in front of us so that we can have what we think we want. After two, four, and even eight or nine hours playing this at a time, how could one help but view existence as a competition in which we have to get what we want by competing and obliterating whatever is in our way?

It is estimated that one billion individuals have downloaded or played this game (Krafton Press Room, 2022). Over one billion individuals, or roughly one-quarter of every beating heart on this earth, have been consciously or unconsciously indoctrinated by this storyline. They have collectively paid obscene amounts to go to that fantasy island wherein they can obliterate, maim, and destroy someone so they can collect, pillage, and hoard the resources that they want. When it is said like this, doesn't it almost sound like training or preparation for the greater capitalistic existence they are to embrace afterward?

Let's take one more. Another one of the highest-selling games that has ever existed has a simple premise. You are a criminal and you will come to a city. You go to crime bosses around the city and get missions assigned to you. Those missions vary greatly but are almost universally dedicated to committing some act of theft or violent crime in order to gain what are most often the material resources that your boss asked you to attain. In the meantime, you can explore an open world wherein you are permitted to pull people out of their cars, beat them with pipes, steal their cars, steal their money, and engage in just about any form of crime that you find to be "amusing" or profitable in any way. Again, this is one of the highest-selling video games that has ever existed worldwide.

The concept of this game glorifies being a criminal. How is a criminal operationalized? As someone who respects no law and takes whatever resource they want at any given time. This is the game. I wish there was more to this plot. But there's not. The storyline is actually much more complex, but playing the game is fairly simple. You simply go to the local gangster and get assigned missions, and carry those missions out. As you continue to carry those missions out, you progress through the story. You perform all manner of exploitation to and despicable acts on the characters to get what you want and need.

Does this sound familiar? It uses the same ideological hegemony that all of the other games do. The pattern begins to become very clear. Most games require the player to ingest and emulate a certain philosophy or belief system about the world that involves the capitalistic concept of pillaging to get your resources while destroying or defeating the competition who are after those resources as well.

These are the themes which mesmerize the generations we raise and that capture the attention of so much of their conscious life and almost all of their recreational life. Then, we debate whether or not this could be harmful for their young minds and their burgeoning thoughts. I will spare the reader the many studies that show a correlation between these games and the player's mental health and how they see the world. Rather, let it suffice to say that it is obvious that these developers and writers of video games are often implicit in the inception of the creation of false idols in our minds.

As one of many evidences of this, let's examine how video games correlate chronologically with gun violence. The first console was created in 1972, and several months later, the second and far more popular console that became widespread came out. This was the inception of video games and they were very simple. They started with games that simulated ping-pong or games wherein you are stuck in a spaceship and are going through an asteroid field and you have a lone weapon to protect the ship. Yet another very popular game was one wherein you are challenged to lead a caravan of settlers from the prairies of Independence, Missouri, to the Willamette Valley in Oregon. The entire premise is survival and it is amongst the first survival games. However, the storyline is based on fact and it provided a challenging and educational way to navigate this new digital world that human beings created for themselves. (Stuart, 2021).

The 1980s followed the lead of the 1970s. The graphics got a lot more sophisticated but, for the most part, the storylines remained simple and straightforward. The first main console gave way to the second, upgraded version, and therefore, we saw the first shift in console systems. That shift brought better graphics and more sophisticated gameplay. For example, probably the most well-known and greatest hit was a simple game where the player fits blocks into other blocks very quickly before new blocks come. That's it. This is what occupied us for hours, and it was innocent and fun. Another huge favorite at the time involved a round, fictional creature with a mouth that was used to eat up little circles very quickly on a board before ghosts who circulated the board as well caught up with you. Another hugely popular game in the 1980s was one of the first and most important and beloved storyline games that involved a tale of chivalry. A fat and lovable Italian and his intelligent and resourceful Italian brother spend their time navigating a kingdom to save the pudgy man's beloved Princess from peril. The enemies throughout all of the series in these games are fantasy characters who were drawn like cartoons and make cartoon noises as they primarily jump on their enemy's heads and bounce off them to kill them. There are no high-powered rifles, bombs, missiles, or any other reality-based weapons. (Stuart, 2021).

Then came the 1990s. Video games, for the most part, continued to maintain innocent storylines even as the previous consoles were taken over by these newer, more sophisticated models. The pair of comedic little Italian boys who were saving that damsel in distress in the form of a princess continued to dominate the gameplay and received the highest ranks of the 1990s. They were followed by a very popular game that was entirely based on fantasy. This game, like the first, is based on the concept of a young boy traveling to distant worlds and defeating a wide range of terrifying monsters in order to save the young princess from the despair she encounters (MacDonald and Stuart, 2021).

However, in the early 1990s video games did become a little darker. All of a sudden, games about ping-pong and about saving the Princess became games about escaping the Nazi concentration camps and killing as many Nazis as you can. One game featured this plot line, and the entire premise of it was to kill more Nazis and more Nazis, but not only Nazis, but the dogs of the Nazis and a variety of other enemies. Obviously, you kill the final Nazi in the end. This game was closely accompanied by another first-person shooter game wherein the premise is that you are a space Marine who spends his time fighting his way through the nether world. Both of these games injected some darkness into the gameplay that was not found in the vast majority of the video games prior to them. They both came out in the early 1990s, and by the end of the 1990s the genre of first-person shooter solidified major new facets in gaming.

Do you know what simultaneously became a major new facet of society? School shootings. By the end of the 1990s, in 1999, the Columbine massacre occurred. An 18-year-old and a 17-year-old walked into the school and murdered 12 students, one teacher, and they wounded 21 additional people. It was the deadliest school shooting in United States history. (The Editors of Encyclopedia Britannica, 2024).

While it was the deadliest, it was far from the only school shooting. Mass shootings and school shootings evolved drastically throughout the latter part of the twentieth century. The data for school shootings is varied and spread out based on the criteria that the researcher uses for school shootings and mass shootings. It is also surprisingly scant. There are very few credible sources that collect cumulative and comprehensive data on school shootings. Using what little information there is, let's start from the 1950s.

In the 1950s, there were 17 incidences of school shootings and in the 1960s, there were 18 instances. Obviously, one instance is an instance too many. However, it becomes clear that during these decades school gun violence was at a relative minimum (Sawhney, 2018).

However, what happens in the 1970s? This amount balloons up to 30 instances (Sawhney, 2018). In other words, there were nearly double the instances of gun violence at school in the 1970's than in the decades previous to it. What changed? The peace and love hippie movement of the 1960s continued into the 1970s. The protests against Vietnam and the concepts of war and hate were generally condemned just the same in the 1970s as in the 1960s. Obviously, this is a complex question that deserves a complex sociological answer that is beyond the scope of this book. However, it seems unsettling that the moment our kids entered a virtual world wherein they could shoot other things, they began shooting each other at much higher rates. There were two games during the 1970s that could be considered first-person shooters. Both had simple plots. One places you in space where you have to shoot enemies and the other forces you to shoot other players to gain points. Neither was bloody or gory or had any kind of realism to them. However, the unconscious concept of shooting another was there.

In the 1980s, the school shootings jump up to 39 in the decade (Sawhney, 2018). Video games are beginning to reach the widespread population and the average boy or girl is playing one of the consoles in this decade. There are still very innocent storylines during this decade and there are still relatively few, if there can be such a thing, school shootings. However, they are climbing and climbing fast.

Then came the 1990s. The innocent and straightforward plot lines become the first-person shooters that serve as a prototype for the ones that we know today. The number skyrockets to 62 incidents of school shootings (Sawhney, 2018). 62 incidences. The 1990s redefined school shootings and it became a widespread concern. Music, as art is so excellent in doing, raised consciousness about this issue in its infancy as it began to take off. The 1990s became the single worst decade for gun violence in schools than any decade in United States history. There can be no doubt that loose gun policies and erroneous beliefs that the Second Amendment should have no guard rails helped drive the phenomenon. The gun lobby, the NRA, and the endlessly feckless and greedy politicians are obviously the primary culprits for the widespread disaster that is this issue. However, video games may have been part of the catalyst that created the culture. Perhaps we learned if we could kill our enemies and take out our frustrations in the video game, we could also do it in real life. 62 incidences of school shootings in the 1990s is the equivalent of more than one shooting in every state. The dread and angst that any parent must have felt during the 1990s while watching their kids get on the bus must have been overwhelming.

The 2000s picked up where the 1990s left off. The number one game was the aforementioned game wherein the protagonist, you, walk around and steal and take whatever material resource you can to appease your boss and keep what was left over for yourself. In the meantime you can kill, hurt, and do a wealth of other unthinkable acts to the characters in a fictional city you inhabit. This is the game that was mentioned before that over 1.7 billion beating hearts on this earth – which is about ¼ of it – have played and purchased and, in many cases may continue to play. This decade also featured three major first-person shooters that would come to dominate the market. All three contain the same concept. You must preserve the way of life and resources of your people and you must kill and destroy the way of life of the enemy. And as always the hegemonic concept and the absurdity that is "it's not murder if it is war" is present in each storyline. Each presents a worldview that it is moral to destroy your enemy in order to preserve your resources, people, and way of life. The central means by which this is accomplished is not by one's mind or by negotiation or by any means other than total physical and mental destruction and annihilation of one's enemy. Therefore, each game becomes kill or be killed and your gun preserves your life. Your gun, in each first-person shooter, and especially in the very widespread and large hits that came out in the 2000s, is implicitly portrayed as your solution and your deliverance. This is a large part of the hegemony that indoctrinates many gamers who pick up the controller and fall into the addiction that is gaming. Your player status in the game, your material welfare, and your strength are all portrayed as things that you can attain with scores and the enforcement of who you are and what you want is accomplished by the force of your gun.

It must be said that during the 2000s, despite these gains, the foot was taken slightly off the gas of violence. Instead, other games full of ideology and indoctrination in the form of hegemony became popular. A major video game that rose to prominence was a game without a storyline. Instead, it featured a made-up family and in the game you control that invented family and create a happy and pleasing world for them. This game, like most video games, speaks directly to the concept of what Freud called the "id," or our base drives and desires. It features a family and the player's objective, if present at all, is finding a way to satiate some of the perceived drives and impulses of that family. Therefore, for most game players, it became a surge of capitalistic greed wherein the players would try to accumulate as much as they could not only from a material standpoint but from a physiological, narcissistic, and especially, as Freud would no doubt appreciate, sexual standpoint. The game features families who are always "DTW," meaning "Down to Woohoo." It is important to note that the rise of this game closely accompanied the rise of the concept of reality television. Therefore, it enabled individuals who saw the false idols of reality television stars brought before them play out those fantasies, misplaced drives, and desires on a miniature stage in much the same way that many young boys act as and pretend to be their favorite football player in football video games or in real life.

Other games tapped into the vanity and narcissism of other celebrities in the 2000s. For instance, one game forced the purchase of a guitar-shaped controller. The premise is that you get to control one of the musicians on the stage of a band that you probably already know and love. In other words, you are one of the people in the band. If you play the notes the correct way, adoration and vanity and fame and wealth come your way. The game predeceases itself entirely on the cultivation of vanity and greed. However, it does depart from the carnage and destruction of killing everything in your path.

Another type of game that did not follow the same model of false idols but created them nonetheless involved sports. Sports games evolved as video games evolved. At first, they were simply a simulation of the sport. You control the batter, quarterback, or other athlete and the entirety of the game was playing the game. Then, slowly, as the game evolved, other storylines and concepts came into it. Sports games integrated the concepts of salary caps and greedy players and other concepts that, while realistic, entered new ideals and drives into the gameplay.

There is one console and set of games during the 2000s that brought sports games back to their purity and mirrored the innocent gameplay of the ping-pong game in the 1970's. These games integrated actual movement rather than sitting and hitting a gamepad. The console featured simple games that were played with a special controller that enabled you to actually swing and punch rather than push buttons that simulated these things. These games were very popular and diverted some of the attention to the games that focused on false idols.

Therefore, it is not surprising that the mass killings during this decade actually declined. The number of school shootings was less, 60, but by no means does this narrative intend to imply that they got easier or less difficult to deal with during the 2000s (Sawhney, 2018). However, it is worth noting the correlation between the minimization of false idols in some of the major games during this decade and the simultaneous reduction of mass killings. The trend in the video game storylines did change. The change was not immense or widespread and for many, it was not even noticeable. However, there were different types of games that were very widely played and accepted and although oftentimes they created other false idols, the violent concepts did reduce for those who played those games.

The Supreme Court of the United States during this decade gave video game companies absolution of any responsibility that their games could cause violent impulses or beliefs in children. However, many doctors and evidenced professionals disagreed. Professor Kenneth Dodge at the Center for Child and Family Policy states, "the evidence is clear that playing first-person shooter violent video games for a long period of time increases the likelihood that a child will behave aggressively, hitting others, bullying others" (Keller, 2022, para. 4). Dr. Michael Rich of the Digital Wellness Lab in Boston's Children's Hospital adds, "What happens is it shifts our center, it shifts what we're sensitive to, it bothers us that guns are involved in conflict resolution" (Keller, 2022, para. 4).

There are a number of studies and concepts that back and support these statements. However, if it's not obvious that a child or an adult playing a video game wherein they get to cheat, steal, manipulate, torture, and ultimately kill can increase that child's violence, what can be called obvious? This is the premise of BF Skinner's or Ivan Pavlov's concepts about conditioning. This is behavioral therapy at its heart. It is classical conditioning. It needs no further proof to make its point. It is part of the same reason that many of the soldiers (who are just slightly older children) we send to war are unable to come back and function at a high level in society without therapy and copious assistance. War is classical conditioning at its worst. And it is costing more lives every day amongst those who are killing and amongst those who are dying. Similarly, video games may be causing more angst and trauma to those who are playing and to those who are not playing alike. They may be creating maladaptive behavioral patterns in those who play and these behaviors put everyone in society on guard.

The killings reduced – relatively – in the 2000s but this reduction did not last long. The upcoming years would see a nightmarish carnage like never before when it came to mass killings in the United States. The problem has never been stalled since the 1970s. However, in the 2000s it was temporarily and very mildly slowed. The false idols that video games help to create would see behemoth proportions in the following decade.

According to The Guardian (2021), the top fifteen games of the 2010s featured ten that were first-person or third-person shooters. Ranking in at number four was another version of the game based on killing, hurting, and stealing anything in sight to please your bosses in a city that looks eerily like New York City, except it focuses on the very worst aspects of it (MacDonald and Stuart, 2021).

One of the crowning achievements in video gaming in the 2010s is a game set in 1911. The main player is a former outlaw. His wife and son have been taken hostage by the American government and are being ransomed for the protagonist's services as a hired gun. In other words, the American government stole your wife and child and said that you must do their bidding and kill who they want you to kill in order for you to get your wife and child back. Your job is then to track and hunt your former gang members in order to be with your wife and child again.

The themes in this game, like so many of the others, indicate and exhibit the hegemony that is at the center of the video game industry. Who is the true enemy in this game? The government. They are the ones who stole your child and wife and they are the ones who ultimately are the antagonist. How does the government function as an antagonist? They force the protagonist, or us, in the allegorical representation, against our old friends who we once cared for and loved. In other words, it pits the people against the people. The game suggests that violence is again the primary way to solve the problem and the gun and force are the true "peacemakers" of the world that the game creates for the user.

Benjamin Triana (2015), an assistant professor at the University of South Carolina Aiken, comments on some of the storyline and what it portrays in this game. He focuses on the concept of what he calls "the terministic screen" (para. 6). He exhibits how the main character uses this screen or logic to justify wrong, evil, or morally questionable actions. In other words, we are playing, and in the game, you are told that you can do bad things for good reasons. If an immoral thing could be justified due to the result that is obtained by doing that thing, it is justifiable. You may remember the first time you heard this logic when Machiavelli said it. There is no substantial difference between this terministic screen and the concept that the ends justify the means.

How does the concept of the ends justifying the means fall into the category of hegemony? It mimics what we are told implicitly and explicitly about how we should conduct ourselves in our economic life. The ends of our wealth or economic well-being are justified by the means of how we get there. If I began listing the dubious characters or outright criminals who are at the top of our economic ladder, I could fill volumes of books. However, in every case, such as the former President who was discussed previously, any indiscretion is forgiven by virtue of the concept of the ends justifying the means. This is why a former President can try to stay in office while defying the will of the people, or any CEO can thwart, manipulate, belittle, and destroy the will of the American worker in the creation of his massive and unending wealth. The culture has created a world in which these actions are permissible. Our video games not only reflect but actively preach it and further it by any means necessary.

Let's examine how the trend of school shootings did during these years of wayward-themed video games. The number shot up to 149, according to the Washington Post (2023). In other words, it skyrocketed. It was during this decade that most of us who lived through it began to become tragically used to hearing about school shootings on the news. This was also the decade in which the Supreme Court decided that the writers of these video game themes and storylines are immune to any type of legislation that would limit what they are calling free speech (Ferguson, 2013).

In other words, the Supreme Court does not believe that any game creator should be limited in any way on the indoctrination and other forms of hegemony that they use to cognitively and behaviorally shape the minds of the young and old alike through their video games. Despite all of the obvious psychological evidence to the contrary, the Supreme Court served as an arm of the ruling class and put no limits on the video games developer's right to indoctrinate us without borders or rules of any type. The Supreme Court ruled this and, to paraphrase Shakespeare in *Julius Caesar*, the Supreme Court is filled with honorable men and women. The fact that, according to CNN as recently as 2018, the United States had 57 times the amount of school shootings than every other industrialized nation combined seems to have no effect on the verdict of the Supreme Court (Grabow et al., 2018). The fact that this number is only growing with every passing day and that children are becoming afraid to go to school in massive numbers and are suffering psychological harm by the fear of more school shootings is of no consequence to the Supreme Court. In the United Kingdom, after a single school shooting in Scotland, their Parliament banned private ownership of most handguns and semi-automatic weapons and requires registration for shotgun owners (Shapiro et al., 2022). Meanwhile, in the United States, the video game company's right to do whatever they want was deemed and remains permissible by the Supreme

Court. But, as we are told, the Supreme Court is filled with honorable men and women.

It seems clear that the United States has many factors for their being enamored with guns. The societal and moral values that are unique to the United States undoubtedly play a large part and perhaps the most significant part in its gun culture. It has an affinity for guns that dates back to the Second Amendment to the Constitution. The concept of having the right to bear arms seems an indelible part of our culture that is never questioned.

Perhaps the obvious solutions of cultural change, gun control, and different video game themes and messages are evaded for other reasons. Perhaps the ruling class wants these false idols to stay in place as the "bread and circuses" that they are. Let's not forget that the video game industry alone was worth around $188 billion last year (2022), which was a year in which net sales actually contracted, according to CNBC (Browne, 2022). Perhaps the hegemony that is easily created by entities like the Supreme Court or other branches of government wants us to keep being occupied with these things on the pretense of catchlines from our Constitution including "free speech" or "for a well-regulated militia, being necessary for the security of a free state, the right of people to keep and bear arms, shall not be infringed" (U.S. Const. 2012, p. 63) The Supreme Court has said that the welfare of the people is less important than the establishment of broad conceptual ideals written down in 1776... a time when life looked nothing like life today. The Supreme Court has said this, and let's never forget, that they are honorable men and women.

The point here is to suggest that there is a clear and obvious financial motive to the government's actions. The Supreme Court is most certainly not any exception to this, and let's not forget that there has never been a Supreme Court justice in modern history who has reflected the socioeconomic status of the very people over whom they so gleefully make laws.

All of the players in the industry of video games have similar interests. The video game makers want to create profit. This is their stated vision, and it is almost undeniable that this is their primary interest. To put this in perspective, Social Security spending in the United States is not the most expensive part of its budget. However, it is a sizable portion and in 2023 its anticipated spending levels, according to the Center on Budget and Policy Priorities (2023), is $1.4 trillion. Therefore, the video game industry is just short of one-third of the cost that it takes to provide a social safety net under every American. Think of the magnitude of that for a moment. What does that say about our values? We are willing to spend about one-third of what we spend to secure our grandparent's well-being or helping those with disabilities on games that tell us to hate our government, that the ends justify the means, and or that violence is the answer to our problems.

Every systemic structure serves to boost and prop up a system that holds these values to be self-evident. There is a cost to these false idols and we are bearing the cost every day. There were six hundred and ninety mass shootings in the United States in 2021, according to CNN (Boschma, 2022). Six hundred and ninety mass shootings occurred! The pace of these shootings is far greater every decade now and that fact is becoming a constant in our society. What is not becoming constant is any movement to change it on any level. As I write this, PBS notes that 2,842 people have been killed in mass shootings in the United States since 2006 alone (Dazio et al., 2023).

In the 2021 study of over 2,263 students by Riehm et al., the researchers considered the psychological effects that school shootings have on children. They found that 38.2% of children were extremely worried about going to school, 31.8% were worried, and 15.2% were stressed. It is obvious that these statistics illustrate that school shootings deter from children's education and impact their development in profound ways. These facts illustrate clinically significant psychological distress that can have lasting effects on children.

Are video games responsible for all this? No. Due to the Supreme Court in its rulings, it becomes extremely hard to know or understand how much of an influence the video games have. However, as it has been evidenced in this chapter, it is clear that video games are created and designed to affect the way we and our children think about the world. It is no different than what any young and developing brain has idolized across any span of time. In the 1960s, teenagers grew up in a world of experimentation and freedom and testing the boundaries of thought and authority, along with playing games like hide and seek, street hockey, and others. These concepts and activities and cultural factors were their video games and, as a result, the 1960s and 1970s saw radical cultural change and togetherness. Conversely, Puritan children in the beginning of our country played with dolls and learned how to make those dolls out of cornhusks and corncobs after being introduced to them by Native Americans (Gorman, 1985). This industry and discipline paved the way for a culture of individuals who valued hard work.

Our children play games about gathering all the money for themselves and killing everything that is in the way of that pursuit. They enjoy and interact with storylines about how much the government uses them and exploits them, and in turn, they have to use and exploit others. They are taught, in the vast majority of games, principles that are used to instill and support selfish means and to create vast inequities in wealth, social justice, and the other avenues of liberty that mimic the society that we have created. This is our design for society and for our children. This, along with an impotent government, creates a cultural structure that seems to forbid the meaningful change that is required of it.

The "bread and circuses" involved in video games is very clear. The systems are, in many ways, indicative of Anthony Burgess's great book, *A Clockwork Orange* (1967). In the book, a totalitarian government tries to 'cure' prisoners by giving them a treatment that deters them from violence. The treatment is meant to brainwash the prisoners and change their impulses through behavioral and cognitive means. Video games are not so overt. They are used implicitly in a way that indoctrinates and brainwashes the child or the adult. They create a virtual world where the rules and the values that are experienced in the physical world are no longer applicable. They prey on our base instincts and drives rather than appealing to our higher thought and higher nature.

For this reason and many others, video games have become a false idol. Video games have become the pillar of many of the existences of our youth and they may be helping to create an army of people who are desensitized to violence, to empathy, and to the basic human drives and instincts that make us truly human – truly humane. As long as they remain the wildly lucrative and endlessly violent and inhumane pacifier that parents so often allow them to be, this false idol will remain a dominant force in shaping the minds and hearts of our future. There is only one certainty that seems clear and that is that history is our guide. That certainty suggests that all of the structures that we have deemed competent to relegate and regulate our society have failed us. Perhaps they all have their own false idols that they worship and are too busy pandering to them to help us save ourselves from ours.

What, then, can prevent us from being endlessly consumed by these false idols that mold our social construction of reality and guide many of our actions? Let's consider how we can free ourselves from the chains of our false idols.

Chapter 9

Critical Thinking

The Cambridge Advanced Leaner's Dictionary (2024) defines education as, "the process of teaching or learning, especially in a school or college, or the knowledge that you get from this" (para 1). According to Lau (2024), the concept of critical thinking is generally credited to the Greek philosopher Socrates, and John Dewey, the American philosopher and educator. This is precisely the concept that would serve to rejuvenate and illuminate democracy regardless of whether all other societal systems fail to do so. Many, many things can be included under the umbrella of education and if education is performed correctly, it seems to utterly safeguard us in the downfall of the Republic.

However, education is not always done correctly and many of our societal systems, and especially our economic system, seem to make the widespread availability to access education and critical thinking skills arduous, at best. Economist Thomas Piketty, in a speech at MIT, said, "rising inequality is highly correlated to unequal access in education," and continued, "In the United States, 95 percent of those with parents at the highest income levels attend college, while only 20 percent of the poorest do" (MIT, 2018). Greater access to education, and especially critical thinking skills, can build greater tolerance to the diversions of false idols. In the United States, the opportunity to build these skills seems to reside inordinately with those who have wealth due to an unfair economic system.

There are a few credible worldwide publications and surveys that would even place the United States in the ballpark of best-educated country. According to *The Balance,* the last worldwide testing occurred in 2018. In 2018, the United States placed 11 of 79 countries in science. It did not place in any of the top five mathematics categories. (Amadeo, 2023) In other words, it is significantly behind. If one can correlate the concept of education with the vitality of a democracy, the United States falls woefully short. The basic concept behind an education is not the mere memorization and understanding of facts and events, procedures and dictums. Rather, education, at its best, should create and promote the aggregate ability to think. It should cultivate critical and intelligent thought. That is what creates a conscientious voter, citizen, and entity that can create and sustain a better society for his neighbor and for himself.

Let's not forget that human beings are animals, just as any other animal in the animal kingdom. We were thrown into this veritable jungle we call the earth and were made to fend for ourselves with what strengths we have. Every animal, in one way or another, contains strengths that have helped them to adapt and persevere in this existence. If the mighty lion did not use its strong, compact body and extremely powerful teeth and jaws to chase and devour other animals, it would probably perish. If it weren't for the ability of the bedbug to remain hidden under almost any circumstance and almost anywhere, it would surely perish from the earth as the pest it is to any animal it encounters.

Similarly, if human beings did not use their great big brains that enable them to reason through and create almost anything that satiates their desires, they would have surely perished long ago as prey to the very physically superior animals that surrounded it. The strongest human, based on physical assets alone, seems to have no chance of winning against the weakest of many of the other animals.

Humanity's strength, then, is intelligence. It is humanity's ability to think critically about the environment they inhabit that is empowering. It is their ability to intelligently examine the environment around them, consider what needs they have to satiate, and then find ways to satiate those needs by manipulating the environment to do so. This is how modern humans have survived, for what National Geographic states have been around 60,000 years (Drake, 2015). In other words, we used our strengths. The only strength that we really have when we compare ourselves to the rest of the animal kingdom is our brains. It is the sole thing that enables us to have such a large extent of dominion and control over the rest of our animal family. It is what brought us the wheel, language, writing, computers, cars, airplanes, and the endless amount of important and life-changing inventions that have populated the entirety of the history of human beings. We are smarter than the rest of the animals. This is what gives us our perceived superiority and nothing more. In his play, *Richelieu* (1839), the great English playwright Edward Bulwer-Lytton wrote, "the pen is mightier than the sword," to signify that writing can be a more powerful tool than violence. In the same way, the brain is a mightier tool than being physically superior. This is our story and this is our strength.

Why, then, do we seem to be idle while this great asset is getting underutilized? False idols derive from psychological weaknesses and desires to find something externally that can fulfill what we are lacking internally. In short, false idols fill a void. It is a psychological void, and it is manipulated by the advertising companies and virtually every other component of the capitalist system around us. They create a false meaning that almost always fills emptiness within us. If we were able to think critically about our actions, drives, and desires, we would find these false idols to be apparitions and meaningless mirages that we chase in lieu of actual meaning in our existence. We would be able to examine the delusion in the false idol that we are worshiping, realize that it is an empty and almost always motive-driven source of deception, and ultimately turn away from it. It would have no power over us if we saw it for all the emptiness and shallowness that it is. If we realized that most of the time, what we were chasing was really just an elaborate hoax that some millionaire or billionaire has created to satiate his own false idol of endless greed, it is almost certain that most of us would turn our backs to it. If we realized and thought critically about the politician's screams about one's group's perceived imperfections being the cause of all our financial woes rather than by changing the 246-year-old system that condemns the masses to live in poverty while the few live in luxury, we could stop the cycle. We could begin destroying and eliminating the concept of the "bread and circuses" that condemn us to the same pattern of distraction and destruction.

Critical thinking about our actions, drives, and desires, then, becomes imperative if we are to be our authentic selves. French historian, philosopher of social sciences, and literary critic René Girard, said, "We don't even know what our desire is. We ask other people to tell us our desires" (Berkowitz, 2024, para. 7). The veracity of this statement becomes increasingly relevant in a society where we chase false idols that are erected for us by maladaptive systems wrought with motives for making them. The solution, then, involves our assertion of authenticity. We must be able to cast aside what we know we don't want and embrace what we actually do want rather than, as Girard stated, ask and mimic others to define what we want for ourselves.

In order to do this, we need to be able to think critically. Our education system takes care of this, though, right? Wrong. There has never been a greater time for critical thinking and yet it would appear that there has never been less critical thinking being taught in our educational system. There has been research from foundations such as the Reboot Foundation and many others that have examined the United States' National Assessment of Educational Progress and found that the concept of critical thinking, let alone an actual class of it, has been extremely inconsistent across states. Furthermore, it tends to be taught and presented less as students get older (Bouygues, 2022).

In other words, for the most part, critical thinking is not being taught as an outright course. How many people reading this can remember their critical thinking class in grade school or high school? The answer is undoubtedly very few. It seems to be entirely state-dependent, and the overall emphasis is put on specific subjects and not the critical thinking that frees us from the irrational belief systems and cognitive errors that you will find on every street corner and in the vast majority of homes in America.

The National Assessment of Educational Progress found that 86% of fourth-grade teachers put "a lot of high emphasis" on critical thinking skills. That number dropped to a mere 39% by eighth-grade (Bouygues, 2022). However, how are these teachers cultivating critical thinking skills if they were never taught them in the first place? It is as if we assume that our teachers have these by virtue of being teachers. However, if critical thinking courses are almost entirely nonexistent in grade school and high school, how can they be learned?

Perhaps it is important to define critical thinking. According to the Foundation for Critical Thinking (2023), critical thinking is, "the intellectually disciplined process of actively and skillfully conceptualizing, applying, analyzing, synthesizing, and/or evaluating information gathered from, or generated by, observation, experience, reflection, reasoning, or communication, as a guide or belief to action" (para. 3). In other words, all disciplines are important. However, for the animal whose brain is the only real means of survival for his existence, critical thinking itself is as important if not more important than any discipline or subject matter that is taught. Despite this, critical thought is left to be gleaned from other subjects and not made to be a subject unto itself. This is a large part of why we have so many false idols, so many "bread and circuses," and continue to lose so many opportunities to grow and find meaning in our lives.

One does not learn to think by thinking. Sure, this is a part of learning to think and it is very important. However, as any philosopher over the ages could surely attest, one learns to think by analyzing thought. The process of analyzing thought is something that we excel at but continue to mitigate in pursuit of other idols. Without the use of critical thinking, we continue to falter and pursue that which is the most appetizing to our senses and hedonistic desires rather than to what is meaningful.

It is this lack of critical thinking and education that sets the stage for the nightmarish play that we continue to watch unfold. When we stop skillfully conceptualizing, applying, analyzing, synthesizing, and/or evaluating information gathered from, or generated by, observation, experience, reflection, reasoning, or communication, we stop using the very thing that gives us the advantages we have over the rest of the animal kingdom. Ralph Waldo Emerson (1967) wrote, in his essay "Self-Reliance" in 1841, "There is a time in every man's life when he arrives at the conviction that envy is ignorance; that imitation is suicide..." Imitation is suicide because it is the cessation of thought. Imitation molds and forges human beings and their beautiful minds into veritable lemmings that will gleefully walk off the cliff of individuality. Every time we follow others, we sacrifice our sense of self. Every time we sacrifice our sense of self, we hand over our ability to think critically. This willful application of our greatest strength as a species has and continues to have devastating consequences.

The concept of the lemming is an important one in regarding thought in general. Lemmings are rodents that live in groups like many animals. There is a popular myth that lemmings as a group jump off of cliffs and commit suicide every year. While this is not true, it is true that lemmings tend to overpopulate whatever habitat they inhabit. When this occurs, they tend to seek out new habitats. Those new habitats often contain new obstacles, such as large bodies of water. They will follow each other across those large bodies of water and there are often many that die trying to follow the other (The Editors of Encyclopedia Britannica, 2023).

The lemming, which tends to prefer very cold weather, serves as a good metaphor for the human being without critical thinking. At some point in the lives of every person who is reading this, we acted and functioned with a lemming mentality. In order to keep up with the pack, or our friends, family, neighbors, and people we looked up to, we sacrificed our better notions to conform with and be a part of the group for whom we had such admiration and faith.

There are easy examples of this for each gender. Men, from a very stereotypical standpoint, often pride themselves on being "strong" and "tough" in a very narrowly defined way. That narrow definition usually includes being able to pick things up and put them down that are very heavy and to endure all types of pain without showing any facial expression or verbal expression that one is actually in that pain. Many men, at some point in their development, can remember a time when they tried to lift the weight of something in order to keep up with or be a part of the larger group who was doing the same. If they critically thought about the absurdity of lifting an inanimate object without any purpose for no other reason but to impress and fit in with a bunch of others for doing the same, there could be no logical argument for it. This is especially true considering the fact that lifting said apparatus quite often resulted in the second manifestation of what often defines "strong" or "tough" in the male value system. In other words, in the act of trying to keep up with the group who is lifting inanimate objects, they often get hurt and then have to act like they are not hurt. As absurd as this paragraph sounds for a thinking being, even as this sentence is being written, it is likely occurring an almost infinite amount of times across the many nations of the world.

Any man (or woman) who participates in this cultural insanity would appear to have lost his or her mind to any outsider who was watching. Furthermore, the man can clearly see this if he steps out of himself, if for only a moment. But he seldom does. Why does he seldom step out of himself? Why does he choose to abdicate the single greatest strength he has? It is due to the fact that he is chasing a false idol. In that moment, when he is asked to perform such ridiculous tasks, he is not seeing the past or how ridiculous his actions are. His mind is only focused on fitting in and belonging. His false idol is vanity. His vanity serves as the distraction to cultivating his greatest asset, which is his mind. When he is unable to lift as much as his friends, he may go home and watch YouTube videos and find others who can help him chase the very thing he thinks he wants – to be able to pick things up and put them down at a rate better than his friends can. These activities become his "bread and circuses" that distract him from anything that is actually important. Like a lemming, he follows the group on whatever journey they take even if it results in the suicide of his intellectual self. Imitation, then, truly is suicide.

Similarly, any woman, from a stereotypical standpoint, usually has a culture that dictates that physical appearance is a very high value in a very narrowly defined way. The herd that she belongs to often has very specifically defined mores and behaviors tailored to how she is able to look. If she wants to retain a subscription to the friends she admires, she believes she will have to dress and make herself up in very specific and often changing ways. If she does not do these things, she suffers being cut off from the herd. Most women, at some point in their development, can likely recall many instances in which they felt pressure to buy clothes, dress, and paint their faces in a variety of different ways to appease the social groups to which they wanted to belong. This drive for belonging, just as with the men, forces them to abandon their own desires.

Any woman (or man) who removed herself from this absurdity and critically thought about it, would likely find it insane. She would likely come to the epiphany that having to portray herself a specific way using specific fabrics and cosmetic products in order to feel 'acceptable' to the society around her has something that is inherently demoralizing about it. She may, if she viewed it from a viewpoint outside of her own, come to the conclusion that there is something intrinsically demeaning to her that she should have to go to such lengths before she could present herself to the society. However, this is not occurring. This is because, like the man, she is chasing a false idol. Her desire to fit in creates the false idol of vanity, too. Her desire to be a part of the herd sacrifices the very thing that she paradoxically is attempting to attain – a stronger sense of self. Since her stronger sense of self, like the man, hinges upon how others see her, she commits suicide of the self.

In a study in *Advances in Physiotherapy* by Bersås et al. (2009), the authors studied gender differences in physical performance tests in young men and young women. Thirty-eight women and twenty-five men did sit-ups and pushed-ups in timed intervals and were evaluated for muscular endurance and power. There was no significant difference between the sexes in the mean number of sit-ups done, while the men performed significantly more push-ups than the women. Given the example of the man and the social norm listed above, regarding physical strength and perceived toughness, this study seems to cast some doubt on the stereotypes and expectations that men are somehow superior physically and that that false belief is justified. Perhaps it calls for an examination of the social construction of these expectations.

This phenomenon is occurring in men and women, children and adults, young and old, black and brown and white in an infinite amount of ways each and every day. Our thoughts are being molded like potter's clay by society and the endless commercial bombardments, images that flood our consciousness, cultural and industrial mores, and endless other ways every day. They are insidious, and they often force or coerce us to commit intellectual suicide and sometimes actual suicide in the same way that a group of lemmings often create an atmosphere wherein other lemmings commit suicide by following the herd. It is our herd instinct that seems to trump our intellectual instinct. This is something that is born of values and nothing more. Our values are shaped by our environment but are wholly created by ourselves. We get to choose what values we have regardless of how many images flood us with however many nefarious or ulterior motives they have. We are ultimately responsible for what values we choose.

Orwell's *1984* once again becomes prophetic. George Orwell created a world wherein every aspect of society and culture pushed individuals to live a certain way. Big Brother was the government and godlike and was able to dictate how the individuals in that society should live. As Orwell illustrates in the book, that social control by Big Brother worked. The society was almost wholly complacent and obedient to the messages and dictates of the world that it created. It can be seen, in some ways, as analogous to our society today, with one major exception. Orwell's government was overt about their control over every aspect of the lives of its citizens. Our societies are not overt at all about the control they exert. Modern-day control by the government and the economic system, which are often intertwined, is covert. It is achieved through subliminal messages, cultural inferences, visual cues, auditory cues, economic hegemony, and so many other ways.

However, Orwell presented a protagonist who resisted the masses. His protagonist, Winston, was the lemming who refused to swim across the lake he knew he could not swim. Winston showed resistance and an unwillingness to do what he was told. He refused to inherit the values of the past in order to belong to the present. He thought critically about the society he was in and how he wanted to fit within that society. He was an individual. As an individual, he asserted his belief systems and views because he was entitled to do so and did not need permission from any other.

We are left with the same dilemma as Winston. We can very easily continue to follow the leader and commit intellectual suicide. The same divisions and corruption, and endless mind-washing will likely continue to occur. Or, we could use our secret weapon. We can use the weapon we have been given for as long as human beings have been on the earth. We can use our brains to think critically about what we want our lives to look like and how we want it to be. This is our primary defense against the false idols and the "bread and circuses" that are present in each and every day.

Chapter 10

The Death of Democracy

The term democracy comes from the Greek word *dēmokratia*. The term can be broken down into dēmos, which means 'people' and the word kratos, which means 'rule.' It is often posited that democracy existed in some form amongst tribes and ancient peoples prior to 500 B.C. However, the actual term democracy was coined in the fifth century B.C. It was coined by the ancient Greeks, who not only used the term but practiced this new form of government in some of its city-states, and especially the city of Athens (Froomkin et al., 2023).

It is conceivable that the concept of democracy in those years may have been as controversial as the concept of communism in the years of Karl Marx. It completely rejected the oligarchy or authoritarian rule by the few that is so prevalent throughout the course of history. New ideas that seem radical are commonly rejected, and one only needs to flip through the pages of any history book to see the rejection and acceptance and utter conflict that new concepts and change bring.

Democracy, or people rule, is supposed to take the power out of the hands of the few and place it into the many. In doing so, it is intrinsically made to ensure that the systems in society, on one level or another, are accountable to the people of that society. President Abraham Lincoln, in his immortal Gettysburg address, summed up this concept extremely well. He stated that, "government of the people, by the people, for the people, shall not perish from the earth" (The Editors of Encyclopedia Britannica, 2024).

This concept and system seem sublime. If we all have a say in how we are governed, then government should always serve at least the majority of us. As long as safeguards are created to protect the minority, this seems to be the making of an equitable and good society – a more perfect union.

However, *seems* is the operative word in the previous sentence. President Franklin Delano Roosevelt, who became president sixty-eight years after Abraham Lincoln, added to Lincoln's concept a note of caution. He stated, "Democracy cannot succeed unless those who express their choice are prepared to choose wisely. The real safeguard of our democracy, therefore, is education… to prepare each citizen to choose wisely and enable him to choose freely are paramount functions of the schools in a democracy" (Roosevelt Institute, 2024, para. 3) In other words, Roosevelt made it clear that having a vote is wonderful, but if it is not an educated vote, an informed vote, it can put the very concept of democracy in peril. The system and design of democracy remain sublime. The Greeks gifted us with a system so brilliant in its efficacy yet simplicity that it could effectively be a system of government for human beings as long as human beings exist. However, if democracy is not utilized by an educated populace who not only understand their interests but advocate for them with their vote, the system begins to decay. Eventually, history repeats itself as it always has and perhaps, both seemingly and tragically, always will.

Aristotle, who existed within two centuries of the birth of democracy, saw the possibility of corruption of democracy from its very inception. In his book *Politics*, he wrote, "The real difference between democracy and oligarchy is poverty and wealth. Wherever men rule by reason of their wealth, whether they be few or many, that is an oligarchy, and where the poor rule, that is a democracy" (Aristotle, 2014, p. 2031). Aristotle, utilizing incredible insight, could see then what has become abundantly apparent not only then, but remains just as true today. Democracy can lose the humanism that it has almost instantaneously the second it turns into oligarchy. What is the mechanism that creates an oligarchy? Money. It was as true in Aristotle's time in the 300s BC as it is now in the information age in the 2000s. If it is not the first false idol, it is amongst the first false idols.

The ancient Greeks utilized a direct democracy. A direct democracy is a democracy wherein each person individually votes on all items that are up for a vote. Therefore, it has no representatives who are elected to conduct the affairs of the government. Each person votes on what affects their life. This is in stark contrast to the modern form of democracy, which is a representative democracy. In a representative democracy, you vote for someone and then trust them to vote for your interests (Schiller, 2024). Representatives, then, should not only think like and advocate for the needs of the people they serve but should ideally be one of the people they serve. They should not only reflect the values and belief systems of who they serve but also the socioeconomic status and hardships of the people who elected them.

Can you think of the last time the United States had a poor person in office? In 2018, the median net worth of any given individual in the Senate was 1.76 million and in the House of Representatives was $510,000 (Statista Research Department, 2024). The current wealthiest person in Congress is a man who has $460 million (Ong, 2023). That is his net worth, and not his gross, which would be even higher. Unlike the income of the regular worker in this country, the incomes of our politicians typically rise. Keep in mind that the current salary that we pay this representative is only $174,000 (Wagner, 2023). The other approximately $459.8 million came from places other than the American people he serves.

This is where Aristotle's insight becomes so poignant. He told us that poverty and wealth make the difference between rule by the few – oligarchy – and rule by the many – democracy. President Franklin Roosevelt's insight adds a warning that illustrates the key variable between what makes a society an oligarchy or a democracy. If the people are not educated to vote in an intelligent way for their interests, an oligarchy will inevitably rise to power. Every time the many in the working class vote against their interests by electing people who don't want unions or to create living wages or legislate for better working conditions for their hard work and labor, this exemplifies what Franklin Roosevelt said. Every time large amounts of individuals vote into office representatives who want to hawkishly pick fights and engage in wars with other countries and people, sending mostly those individuals to war or to be in harm's way, this exemplifies Roosevelt's statement.

Enough of these scenarios depict a world wherein Aristotle could not have been more insightful. The hegemony and lack of education that manipulates the masses into voting in certain ways erodes democracy the way moving water erodes a rock. It is slow but steady and, over time, extremely effective. It is all based on two major and very manipulative psychological techniques. The first is the "bread and circuses" that Juvenal discussed and the second is the false idols that are worshipped in such a way that renders the population unable to see their own interest. They are weaved into the deception and façade that lies behind every vote that lacks self-interest, like snakes weaving themselves around the minds of the masses.

According to an NPR/Ipsos poll that was published on January 3, 2022, 64% of Americans believe the United States democracy is in crisis (Rose, 2022). In another poll conducted by NBC News on September 27, 2022, it said that 61% of one party did not believe that President Biden won the election legitimately (Murray, 2022). Obviously, massive amounts of distrust and disbelief in American democracy have been created since the 2020 election. This age-old form of government that was meant to ensure the power of the masses could create and better their own existence. It has worked successfully and extremely efficiently since at least the sixth century B.C. But it has suddenly found a great stumbling block in 2020.

Belgium philosopher Mark Coeckelbergh echoes this sentiment that distrust in democracy has been created but not only in America, but democracies in general. In an interview for El País newspaper in Spain, Coeckelbergh stated, "…I think this combination of weak democracies, capitalism, and technology is dangerous" (Figuls, 2023). He further discusses how our democracies are not full democracies, and that our majority voting is too vulnerable to populism and not does not have enough participation (Figuls, 2023).

Why doesn't it have enough participation? Did human beings in the Western world decide to return to the days of monarchs and emperors? Did people forget how to vote and go to the polls and engage in their civic duty?

Nope.

An obnoxiously arrogant man who is only known to the American people because he was born into wealth and got lucky in his business dealings is a poor loser. He cried about losing and pointed and screamed and told other people that the other player didn't play fair. His actions were no different than any toddler in any school or playground in America who lost a game and could not handle the fact that he lost. There was no evidence and there continues to be no evidence that the other guy cheated. So he just plain lied. While this nefarious effort did not destroy democracy, it did more to destroy it than anything that has ever occurred in the past in the country that this same man states he loves. He then proceeded to convince his most ardent believers to violently storm the United States capital as if that would bring the spoiled child his 'toys' back and thereby put him back in the presidency. Despite every attempt, it didn't work. But sadly, it almost did.

This is not, however, really about a poor loser who occupied the White House and ran one of the most powerful countries in the world. This is about the people, who allowed the integrity of their system to be questioned on an utter absence of logic. How could a country utilize 243 years of democracy as a form of government and in year 244, forget the integrity of the system that always delivered it a more perfect union?

According to Levitsky and Ziblatt (2020), there are two basic norms that are essential to democracy. The first they identify as mutual toleration which essentially states that one will accept losing out of respect to the other person they are running to beat. The second norm is forbearance. They talk about how an elected representative not utilizing all the power they have in any given situation is a large part of what enables democracy to go forward. They go on to state that the endless polarization of our system is creating a divide that is making democracy more and more difficult to continue to sustain. They warn of continued destruction if the polarization and hate continue to grow and spread throughout the American populace at the rates it had been, especially since 2016. Due to the events on January 6, coupled with the increased divisiveness of ideological views within the country between right and left, all of the criteria that contribute to a healthy democracy are missing in the United States at present. This fact creates a perilous situation for a country that is flirting with systemic destruction. It is looking down the barrel of oligarchy if it is not already there.

As one examines history, and history of democracy in particular, the pattern of the loss of forbearance and mutual toleration are just the first steps to the decay of democracy. In a separate publication, authors Levitsky and Ziblatt (2017) examine the history of the death of democracy in different nations across the world. They noted that 75% – three out of four – democracies failed in the past due to violent overthrow, or coup d'état, prior to the Cold War. This still occurs occasionally, as in the case of Thai's Prime Minister Yingluck Shinawatra in 2014. This looked a lot like the January 6 insurrection, wherein there was a violent attempt to overthrow, or in that particular case, keep in place, the current regime. The Egyptian president Mohammed Morsi is another example of a violent coup d'état which occurred as recently as 2013 and was successful. It is important to note that the United States had their violent insurrection and coup d'état as recently as 2021. This is another major indicator that the democracy in the third most populous nation in the world is faltering.

However, these authors note that these overt and violent denials and overthrows of democracy are becoming increasingly rare in current times. Since the Cold War, the demise of democratic institutions has occurred largely at the hands of the very politicians who were the beneficiaries of that democratic system. The days of military leaders overthrowing democracy by force have declined since the Cold War. The degradation of democracy has become far more insidious, and the politicians who enact that degradation use far more covert tools. Hungary's Victor Orban used his popularity to pack the courts with judges who found ways to change the Constitution and other rules to weaken his opponents. The democratically elected Hugo Chavez in Venezuela used his power to create an unfair playing field for his opponents by packing the courts, blacklisting his enemies, pushing through legislation that would allow him to stay in power indefinitely, and bullying any independent press. This has occurred to varying extents in the United States, in Venezuela, Hungary, Ecuador, Peru, Georgia, the Philippines, Poland, Russia, Sri Lanka, Turkey, Ukraine, and the list keeps going. (Livitsky and Ziblatt, 2020) This is the new democracy shaped and coddled by vain little men who covet power like the false idol that it is. This is the new way that people's voices get thwarted and is the new way we lose sight of people's rule.

The United States has begun to walk down the same dark path that these other countries have walked. The path, as Shakespeare (1994) said of death in *Hamlet,* may be, "an undiscovered country from which no traveler returns" (Shakespeare, 3:1.81-82). Once democracy turns into a dictatorship or oligarchy, it is not an easy path back. Just ask the 75% of countries who violently overthrew their leaders prior to the Cold War. Leaders, such as the one that America elected in 2016, who have no regard or adoration for the Greek institution of democracy or for the concept of people ruling in general, are anathema to the health and continued existence of not only democracy, but the well-being of the Republic itself.

The issue, as it often does, comes down to the concept of hegemony. The ruling class, or patricians, in the United States or any country, sets the discourse, values, and norms by which the plebeian or working class live. How do they do this? They hold the microphone. Why do they hold the microphone? Because they own the microphone, the people who made the microphone, the presses, the publishing companies, the newspapers, radio companies, the social media companies, and every other means by which words and messages can be produced to influence other human beings. The masses are, therefore, effectively brainwashed and fed beliefs and values that are most often completely against their very interests.

One only has to listen to any anti-democratic politician with a discerning ear to know that they are serving two masters. As noted, very few, if any, of their salaries, incomes, or net worth match the income that they derive from the job that for which we pay them. The fact that those two masters exist creates an impossibility of them serving both. Tragically, the false idol of greed becomes more appealing than the basic and beautiful human impulses of magnanimity and justice in serving others.

For example, the very concept of trickle-down economics is based on the concept of hegemony. Trickle-down economics is a concept that became popular in the 1980s during the Reagan administration. It is essentially the concept that the Britannica Dictionary (2023) calls, "an economic theory which says financial benefits and advantages given to wealthy people, corporations, etc., will improve the economy and eventually help the poor people in society" (para 1). In other words, the Reagan administration, the Bush administration, and many others in American history decided to sell the American people on the concept that if you give all of the money and breaks to the wealthiest among us, it will somehow benefit you. Could there be a more absurd notion than this? It is reminiscent of a bully at school who goes to all of his classmates and says, "Listen, if you all give me all of your lunch money every day, I'll make sure you don't get beaten up. This will benefit both of us – I protect you, and you give your money to me. We both win." Of course, the only person that the classmates ever had to worry about was him beating them up.

In a 2020 study conducted by David Hope and Julian Limberg of The London School of Economics and Political Science, the authors studied the effect of trickle-down economic policies amongst 18 market-based economies in OECD countries. They found that policies that reduced taxes on the rich lead to tremendous income inequality, with the few having everything and the many having very little. They also found that the tax cuts for the rich do not have any significant impact on employment or economic growth. (Hope and Limberg,

2020) In other words, there is no claim to suggest that it works to improve the lives of the many. There is an undoubted claim and undeniable proof that it improves the lives of the few who profit from the tax cuts.

Trickle-down economics, which also can be called supply-side economics, are much older than any of these political figures. And the concept is also probably much older than the United States or any contemporary country. The concept is likely as old as human beings. It is a psychological way for one group to dominate the other. It is a way to create an artificial value system and belief system that opposes the interests of the very people who are asked to believe it. This is the way that democracies are eroded and destroyed today. If everybody listens to and believes in the veracity of supply-side economics, then corporations, millionaires, and billionaires continue to get richer and control more of the goods and other means in society. The working class continues to get poorer and gets used to struggling in even more horrible working conditions. They eventually learn to blame themselves because they are told they are not working hard enough because if they did work hard enough they could be one of the dominating classes. This is also hegemony. And it is the single largest destroyer of democracy in the modern world. It thwarts the people's will through brainwashing and other ideological red herrings and false idols.

Let's examine a non-politician example of this hegemony that destroys democracy. The Brookings Institution is an American research group that was created in 1916. It claims to be nonpartisan and performs a public service of generating valuable research for our society (Brookings Institution, 2024). It releases publications demonstrating this research for public consumption. On January 4, 2022, William A. Galston and Elaine Kamarak of the Brookings Institution published an article entitled, "Is democracy failing and putting our economic system at risk?" They proceed to argue that American democracy is moving toward failure, that this democratic failure puts the economic system, capitalism, at risk, and then go on to detail what private markets could do given these threats to the capitalist system. Especially pertinent is Rebecca Henderson, who is from the Harvard business school, and her quote at the inception of the article. It reads, "I think the decline of democracy is a mortal threat to the legitimacy of capitalism" (Galston and Kamarak, 2022, para 1).

This article was chosen because of the nonpartisan nature of the author. It would be very easy to choose a partisan media outlet that creates hegemony that undermines democracy. But this was meant to be nonpartisan.

The entire thrust of the thesis of this article focuses on the economic system, the markets, in short: the money. The conception that the reader takes from it is that saving our economic system is number one, and in order to do that, we have to fix the small matter of democracy. The value, then, becomes financial.

It stresses that material wealth is the primary value and that the concept of people rule is secondary or even tertiary. In fact, the antagonist is presented as the democracy, and the economic system is the protagonist. In short, one could easily come away as viewing the material world as having full primacy as the greater objective in the world when juxtaposed to the people's rule – the democracy. The article creates another red herring that takes our eyes off the true ball of people's rule and the greater good for society.

As evidenced, our democracy is in trouble. It is in trouble because of the greed and desire for power that permeates it. It is in trouble due to the lack of respect and interest in maintaining it. It is in trouble due to the insidious attempts by those who enter into politics manipulating us into selling it or giving it away, or even abolishing it altogether. Many of the concepts that have been created and used to deter us from our interest utilize the psychological means of manipulation and especially distraction. These methodologies and manipulations have become increasingly insidious and tragically, they have also become increasingly effective. All of those methods and methodologies depend on the concept of "bread and circuses." Everything that the ruling classes use to deter us and occupy our minds is distractions. This is not a new phenomenon and can date back to as long as human beings exist. However, the fact that it is not losing its efficacy in time forewarns the possibility of disaster for humanity.

Fortunately, we have all of the tools and resources to thwart this oncoming storm at our disposal. As noted, President Franklin Roosevelt realized what cannot be denied. He told us that education is the true safeguard of society. As anti-Democratic leaders have taken office in the United States, education rates have plummeted. The anti-democratic leaders also tend to be the least educated leaders. As a result of their policies and values, the emphasis on education has often dropped dramatically. In 2022, there were more than one million fewer students in college than in 2019. That is an approximate drop of 13% in attendance. Community colleges are seeing the sharpest drop but four-year colleges are not far behind (Nadworny, 2022).

If education continues to be suppressed, then it seems likely that the oligarchs are getting what they want. Less education equals less democracy. Less democracy equals less humanity. Without democracy and without humanity, we sit perched on the ledge of history, waiting for it to repeat itself. It recalls what Roosevelt said, "Democracy cannot succeed unless those who express their choice are prepared to do it wisely" (Roosevelt Institute, 2024).

How can those express their choice wisely if they do not have the knowledge to do so? How can they make decisions on their own and in the best interest of the common good if they do not have the information or thinking skills to make those decisions? The game that is played in contemporary democracy is a rigged one. There are very few who get to paint the picture and then turn and ask the great many to tell them what they see. Without education for the many, they will only see what is being presented on the surface and are not able to interpret the picture to analyze its deeper meanings. We will just vote on the immediate information. For any lover of literature, it may be easy to conceive of this by recalling a great Robert Frost (1995) poem. Most of us have heard of "Stopping by Woods on a Snowy Evening." On the surface, it seems like a straightforward moment in time wherein the speaker of the poem is in the woods with his horse. The two beings pause for a moment and take in their surroundings. However, on deeper analysis, the poem becomes a deep, thoughtful, and introspective examination of death. If the participants of a democracy are increasingly unable to investigate the deeper meaning of the messages they receive, they become malleable and are manipulated by the messages of the oligarchs. This is the ultimate danger to democracy that is pervasive and ever present. It is with "bread and circuses" that we continue to be deterred from seeing what really matters to us and chasing what we value. However, the power lies within us. It lies within us as long as the ancient Greek definition of the word democracy remains true. It seems the gap can only be filled by illuminating the splendor that is education.

Postscript

Several weeks went by in Syracuse and the warm spring air underwent its seasonal metamorphosis and became hot and humid summer air. Chris became increasingly tired of his schedule and of all that detracted from what he loves. He thought about his life and he thought about his position in the world and the thoughts he had gave way to more thought. These thoughts began to affect the way he saw the world.

One warm and windy summer night, he got into his car to drive home from his job as an appliance salesman after another tiring day of work for which he was woefully underpaid. As he started his drive, he saw a billboard for a beer company with a seductive woman drinking a beer in an alluring pose as she used her other hand to clear the ice off of the name of the beer behind her. Chris glanced at the billboard as he continued to drive.

He then turned on the radio. He heard an upbeat and soft female voice state,

"Are you leaving the first footprint on Mercury? Are you jogging in an open field? Or, are you about to pull off the greatest bank robbery of the century? Are you in your car? Or, are you praying that the predator in the forest can't see you? A voice in your ear can take you anywhere. Buy our audiobooks and be delivered from your boring car rides."

Chris smiled and shook his head. He reached over to the touch screen and turned the station off. He navigated the local classic rock station. On the station, the song "Break on Through" by The Doors was playing. A pleasant look came over his face and he began to sing along jovially with the music. Each time a commercial came on, he switched it to another station. He listened with interest to a half-inning of the Mets as they began playing against the Phillies in an NL East match-up. He listened to the game avidly and when a commercial came, he turned it off.

The warm summer air whipped through the car and tousled his hair as he drove. He focused on the air as it swam around him and provided relief to the sweltering heat of the summer day. He made sure that all four windows were down so that there was a constant flow of fast and breezy air that he felt the entire ride.

On the ride, Chris thought about his family. He thought about how grateful he was to have them. He thought about all the things that he wanted to give them and the hopes that he had for his life with Joelle and Dominic. He dreamed of creating a world with them that would deliver him from the world that was created around him. He conceived of all kinds of plans and dreams that they could have together. Where their dreams and goals departed from his, he would find common ground, and he thought that if this compromise was followed, they could create their own meaningful world together.

Chris pulled up to the school where his son attended. Several moments later, Dominic knocked three times on his window. The knocking startled Chris.

"It's open!" Chris said.

Dominic opened the door immediately. "Thanks Dad."

"You scared me to death!" Chris said with a smile.

"I was trying to scare you to death, Dad. It makes me laugh every time," Dominic said and smiled a mischievous smile as he put his hand through his brown hair.

Chris smiled and began driving home. They continued to listen to the baseball game and switched it off to listen to classic rock whenever there was a commercial.

"How do you listen to this old man music?" Dominic asked.

"It's the music I love, Dom. One day, believe it or not, your kids are going to ask you how you listen to the old man music you like. That's that terrible pop stuff that you like now, you know?"

"I don't think so, dad. I'll never get to be old like you. You're ancient."

"We'll see little buddy," Chris said and smiled as he looked at the road.

They continued to drive and to listen to the game. After a while, Dominic stated,

"Did you think about getting me the Mokata VN phone? I *really* need it, Dad. Everyone else has it at this point and it's embarrassing."

Chris took a deep breath before responding, "I actually have been thinking about that phone. I've been thinking about a lot of things, Dom. And I'm sorry, buddy, but I can't get you the phone."

Dominic's eyes welled with tears. "But Dad –!"

"Now hold on and hear me out," Chris said as he pumped his right hand with his palm open toward Dom and drove with his left hand. "If I got you that, in two months, it will be another phone. And then it will become another pair of jeans. Then it will be this video game and then that video game. In other words, it'll never end! This has already begun and has been happening for a long time. Whatever the newest ad says you should get and whatever your friends say is the cool thing to buy, you're addicted to."

"Well of course I am, Dad. That's how it works!"

"But is that how it *has* to work, Dominic? The cell phone isn't important, and neither is a video game or anything else you think you must have. The more that you buy into the concept that these are things that are important, the less you're going to *really* have. It will just become one big competition wherein whoever has the most resources, wins. What if we try something different?"

"What do you mean, different?"

"What if we focus on what is really important to you rather than what you think is important?"

"The phone is what is important, Dad!"

"I'll tell you what. I'm going to list some things that I think might even be more important than your phone to you. If I name one that you like, I'll get it for you. How's that?"

"Good luck Dad. Sometimes I think you're crazy."

"What if I took you to the ocean this summer? Would that be better than a cell phone? You'd be able to sit on the beach and see the water and have a solid week or two out there."

Dominic sat in the passenger seat and thought for a few moments. Then he said,

"I love the ocean and I would love to do that Dad, but no deal. That doesn't equal the Mokata cell phone."

"You're a difficult sell," Chris said as the wind whipped through his hair. "How about you and I go camping in the gorge and we go out on the boat and enjoy the lake for a weekend or two this summer?"

"You're getting warmer Dad, but that's still not worth the cell phone."

"I'm not going to pretend I'm not a little hurt by that one," Chris replied. He listened to the batter who was up at the plate crack the ball with the bat as he thought a few moments.

"What if I took you and Mom to Niagara Falls this year? You'd feel the crashing of the waterfall and the mist on your face. And after that, we'll camp in the Thousand Islands in Alex Bay. And to cap it all off, we'll spend a few nights at Lake Ontario. That's three beautiful places all in one trip. What do you think of that?"

There was a pause for a few moments before Dominic responded. "Will you take me out on a boat on the Great Lake?" Dominic said and as he said it his eyes were as large as saucers.

"I will even let you sit with me at the head of the boat," Chris said and smiled a wide and happy smile.

The moments that followed were saturated with expectation. Chris continued to drive toward their home and Dominic sat very pensively as he looked out the window. Finally, after several minutes, Dominic replied.

"I can't believe I'm saying this, but you got a deal Dad. The Falls and Alex Bay and Lake Ontario for a Mokata cell phone. Deal."

Chris extended his right hand out to his son and his son shook it. "You got a deal," he said. "And I'm proud of you. You just challenged the world around you by not doing what everybody else says you should do. That takes courage, buddy. I'm proud of you."

Dominic nodded but didn't seem to hear his Dad. He was lost in thought about being at the head of the boat on Lake Ontario with his dad.

Chris parked the car. He and his son walked up the old steps and into the door.

"Mom, I'm going to get to be co-captain of the boat!" Dominic said as he ran to his Mother and embraced her tightly. Joelle was preparing dinner in the kitchen when Dominic walked in with Chris.

"That's great, honey!" Joelle said as she hugged her son and her blonde hair fell down onto his head and rested on his shoulders. As she said this, her blue eyes looked at Chris and she smiled a bright, white smile.

"Why don't you go change and begin to do your homework and will talk all about it over dinner?" Joelle asked her son. He turned around and went into his room immediately.

"What's that about?" Joelle asked.

"I'll explain. Can you put dinner on hold for a minute so we can talk at the table?" Chris responded.

Joelle complied and turned the oven off and sat with her husband.

"I'm tired, Joelle."

"Tired of what?"

"I'm tired of listening to everything else and neglecting what is important and what we value. I'm tired of feeling more like a soldier who is following orders than a person who is living for themselves. I'm tired of chasing things I don't want and stockpiling things that I don't need. I want to start focusing on what's important in our lives. We are barraged with images and voices telling us what is and is not important and on what we should be chasing and spending our time and money. I want to focus on what is actually important to me and to you and Dominic. And then I want to spend all of my waking breaths trying to make sure that each of us can find the things that we truly want, rather than the things that we are told we should want. I want to not always feel like whatever I have is not enough and that I need to accumulate, accumulate, and accumulate some more, or emulate, emulate, and emulate some more in order to feel whole. When I do feel whole, I don't want it to feel fleeting because the goalposts are constantly being moved and I'm being told that I have to accumulate or emulate more after that. What I'm saying, Jo, is that I just want us to make our own goals instead of chasing the goals of the world around me."

"You don't feel you're doing that now?"

"No!" Chris said emphatically. "I feel like I spend my life occupied with distractions and infatuated with chasing nothings. All I actually need is you, Dom, and enough resources for us to live meaningful lives. The rest is up to us, individually, and as a whole. I'm tired of all the noise and static of the society around us pulling us in every direction. I'm tired of being part of it but I feel like I have to be. I think we can be part of it without being a part of it, you know what I mean?"

"Not exactly."

"I mean we can hear the noise but not listen to it. We can be a part of the world without having to bend our knees and conform who we are and what we want. I mean we can rebel against the dictates of the systems that serve as puppeteers and stop acting like living puppets. I'm tired of worshiping whatever god serves their interests best. I'm tired of us spending so much time pursuing our own false gods that we spend less and less time together enjoying what's really important – us. I promised our son that we will take him to Niagara Falls and Lake Ontario and Alex Bay because they are meaningful places to him that will conjure beautiful memories. If I bought the cell phone, he would just be keeping up with the Joneses and the only true beneficiary of that transaction is Mokata. I want us to live different lives. I know that that is not my call because I can only control my own. But I'm asking you to join with me."

"Honey, I support you. I'm not against any of these things you are saying. I think it will be very hard."

"It will be hard. But the sacrifices will only be hard at first. After that, I think they will become easy. It's just changing a way of life."

"You sound like a philosopher."

"That's well put. Maybe we can all be philosophers. Plato talked about a 'philosopher king.' He said that a king should apply philosophy in the exercise of power. That has only happened a few times throughout history. What's more practical is a philosopher citizen. If we had many people who would utilize critical thought in the exercise of their existence, the whole system would change. So yes, I hope I am a philosopher but I hope you will be one, too. I hope we can be philosopher citizens. Because if we could all be philosophers, and think critically, we could stop chasing what doesn't matter, and start focusing on what does."

References

Amadeo, K. (2023, March 26). *U.S. Education Rankings Are Falling Behind the Rest of the World*. The Balance. https://www.thebalancemoney.com/the-u-s-is-losing-its-competitive-advantage-3306225

Allman, B. (2022). *Socioculturalism*. Education Research: Across Multiple Paradigms. https://edtechbooks.org/education_research/socioculturalism

Ancient Roman Entertainment. (2023). Wabash.edu. http://persweb.wabash.edu/facstaff/royaltyr/AncientCities/web/bradleyj/Project%201/Games.html#:~:text=Men%20all%20over%20Rome%2

Anselme, O. & Robinson, M.J.F. (2013). What motivates gambling behavior? Insight into dopamine's role. *Frontiers in Behavioral Neuroscience, 7*. https://doi.org/10.3389/fnbeh.2013.00182

Aristotle (2014). *Complete Works of Aristotle, Volume 2: The Revised Oxford Translation*. Princeton University Press.

Aurora, K (2023, November 23). The gaming industry: a behemoth with unprecedented global reach. *Forbes*. https://www.forbes.com/sites/forbesagencycouncil/2023/11/17/the-gaming-industry-a-behemoth-with-unprecedented-global-reach/

Barberá, P., Gohdes, A. R., Iakhnis, E., & Zeitzoff, T. (2022). Distract and Divert: How World Leaders Use Social Media During Contentious Politics. *The International Journal of Press/Politics*, 0(0). https://doi.org/10.1177/19401612221102030

Barberá, P., & Zeitzoff, T. (2017). The New Public Address System: Why Do World Leaders Adopt Social Media? *International Studies Quarterly, 62*(1), 121–130. https://doi.org/10.1093/isq/sqx047

Barbu, D. (2022). The invention of idolatry. *History of Religions, 61*(4), 389–418. https://doi.org/10.1086/718968

Barletta, Michael (1998). "Chemical Weapons in the Sudan: Allegations and Evidence" (PDF). *The Nonproliferation Review*. 6 (1): 116–117. https://doi.org/10.1080/10736709808436741

BBC News. (2015, January 10). *Would you be beautiful in the ancient world?* BBC News. https://www.bbc.com/news/magazine-30746985

BBC News. (2019, December 17). *Samsung chairman Lee Sang-hoon jailed for union sabotage*. BBC News. https://www.bbc.com/news/world-asia-50820444

Benson, C. (2023, December 4). *Child Poverty Rate Still Higher than for Elder Populations but Declining*. United States Census Bureau. Retrieved June 22, 2024, from https://www.census.gov/library/stories/2023/12/poverty-rate-varies-by-age-groups.html

Berkowitz, R. (2024, April 28). *Renee Girard and the Internet Influencers*. https://hac.bard.edu/amor-mundi/rene-girard-and-internet-influencers-2024-04-28

Bersås, E., Thomas, E.M., Sahlberg, M., Augustsson, S.R., Augustsson, J. & Svantesson, U. (2009). Gender difference and reliability of selected physical performance tests in young women and men. *Advances in Physiotherapy, 11*(2), 64-70. https://doi.org/10.1080/14038190801999679

Boettke, P. J. and Heilbroner, Robert L. (2023, October 19). *capitalism.* *Encyclopedia Britannica.* https://www.britannica.com/money/topic/capitalism

Boon, S. D., Lomore, C.D., (2006, January 10). Admirer-Celebrity Relationships Among Young Adults: Explaining Perceptions of Celebrity Influence on Identity, *Human Communication Research*, 27 (3), 432–465. https://doi.org/10.1111/j.1468- 2958.2001.tb00788.x

Boschma, J. (2022, November 23). Mass shootings in the US: 2022 could be the second-highest year. *CNN.* https://www.cnn.com/2022/11/23/us/2022-mass-shootings-tracking-second-highest/index.html

Bourne, J. (2020, March 31). *Online advertising: A history from 1993 to the present day [infographic].* Marketing Tech News. https://www.marketing technews.net/news/2013/sep/11/online-advertising-history-1993-present-day-infographic/

Bouygues, H. L. (2022, August 17). *Critical Thinking Skills Not Emphasized By Most Middle School Teachers. Forbes.* https://www.forbes.com/sites/helen leebouygues/2022/08/17/critical-skills-not-emphasized-by-most-middle-school-teachers/?sh=399a266d2ee4

Browne, R. (2022, July 7). *Video game sales set to fall for first time in years as industry braces for recession.* CNBC. https://www.cnbc.com/2022/07/07/video-game-industry-not-recession-proof-sales-set-to-fall-in-2022.html

Brookings Institution. (2024, April 30). About us. *Brookings.* https://www.brookings.edu/about-us/

Bruell, A. (2020, August 20). *Viacom CBS Seeks About $5.5 Million for 30-Second Commercial Spots in 2021 Super Bowl.* Retrieved February 5, 2023, from https://www.wsj.com/articles/viacomcbs-seeks-about-5-5-million-for-30-second-commercial-spots-in-2021-super-bowl-11597956492

Burgess, A. (1967). *A Clockwork Orange.* W.W. Norton & Co. Inc.

Bursztynsky, J. (September 27, 2021). *TikTok says 1 billion people use the app each month.* CNBC. https://www.cnbc.com/2021/09/27/tiktok-reaches-1-billion-monthly-users.html

Business Connect Magazine. (2023, October 18). *Top 10 most followed Facebook Pages in 2023. Business Connect Magazine.* https://businessconnectindia.in/facebook-pages-everyones-talking-about/#google_vignette

Cambridge University Press. (2023). Diversion. In *Cambridge Advanced Learner's Dictionary and Thesaurus. Retrieved September 7, 2024 from* https://dictionary.cambridge.org/dictionary/english/diversion

Cambridge University Press. (2024). Education. In *Cambridge Advanced Learner's Dictionary and Thesaurus. Retrieved September 7, 2024 from* https://dictionary.cambridge.org/dictionary/english/education

Camus, A. (1951). *The Rebel: An Essay On Man in Revolt.* Vintage International.

Carpenter, A. (2022, May 26). *Opportunity Cost Definition.* U.S News. Retrieved April 26, 2023, from https://money.usnews.com/investing/term/oppo rtunity-cost

Cashman, G. (1999) *What Causes War? An Introduction to Theories of International Conflict.* Salisbury, MD: Lexington Books.

Chaucer, G. (2005). *The Canterbury Tales: In Modern Verse.* Hackett Publishing Company.

Center on Budget and Policy Priorities.(2023). *Policy basics: Where do our federal tax dollars go?.* https://www.cbpp.org/research/policy-basics-where-do-our-federal-tax-dollars-go

Choi, S. M., & Rifon, N. J. (2007, March 7). *Who Is the Celebrity in Advertising? Understanding Dimensions of Celebrity Images.* Wiley Online Library. https://onlinelibrary.wiley.com/doi/abs/10.1111/j.1540-5931.2007.00380.x

Chomsky, N. (2016). *Who Rules the World.* Hamish Hamilton.

Clines, F.X., & Myers, S.L. (1998, December 17). Attack on Iraq: The Overview; Impeachment Vote in House delayed as Clinton Launches Iraq Air Strike, Citing Military Need to Move Swiftly. *The New York Times. https://www.nytimes.com/1998/12/17/world/attack-iraq-overview-impeachment-vote-house-delayed-clinton-launches-iraq-air.html*

Cilliers, L. & Retief, F. (2010, March). *Causes of Death among the Caesars (27BC-AD 476).* Acta Theologica. 26. 10.4314/actat.v26i2.52565. https://www.ajol.info/index.php/actat/article/view/52565#:~:text=During%20the%20Early%20Empire%2055battlefield%20(5%20versus%20none)

Collins Dictionary (2023). *Synonyms of Idol.* In Collinsdictionary.com dictionary. Retrieved February 15, 2023. Collins American English Thesaurus https://www.collinsdictionary.com/us/dictionary/english-thesaurus/idol

Cuan-Baltazar, Y., Muñoz-Pérez, M. J., Robledo-Vega, C., Pérez-Zepeda, M. F., & Soto-Vega, E. (2020). Misinformation of COVID-19 on the Internet: Infodemiology study. *JMIR Public Health and Surveillance, 6*(2), e18444. https://doi.org/10.2196/18444

Cuello-Garcia, C., Pérez-Gaxiola, G., & van Amelsvoort, L. (2020). Social media can have an impact on how we manage and investigate the COVID-19 pandemic. *Journal of clinical epidemiology, 127,* 198–201. https://doi.org/10.1016/j.jclinepi.2020.06.028

Dazio, S., & Fenn, L. (2023, April 21). *Mass shootings in U.S. On a record pace in 2023 so far.* PBS News Hour. Retrieved April 25, 2023, from https://www.pbs.org/newshour/nation/mass-shootings-in-u-s-on-a-record-pace-in-2023-so-far

Dickens, C. (2003). *Stories for Christmas.* Platinum Press Inc.

Drake, N. (2015, September 11). Human Evolution 101. *History.* https://www.nationalgeographic.com/history/article/human-evolution-101

Drake, P., & Miah, A. (2010). The cultural politics of celebrity. *Cultural Politics: An International Journal, 6*(1), 49–64. https://doi.org/10.2752/175174310x12549254318746

Elkins, K. (2019, September 30). *29% of Americans are considered 'lower class'—here's how much money they earn.* CNBC. https://www.cnbc.com/2019/09/28/how-much-the-American-lower-class-earns.html

Emerson, R. W., 1803-1882. (1967). Self-reliance. White Plains, N.Y.: Peter Pauper Press.

Ekanem, F.E. (2014). *The Socratic "Man Know Thyself" and the Problem of Personal Identity*. African Journals Online. *Vol. 15* (no. 1) pp. 69-73

Featherly, K. (2023, September 10). *ARPANET. Encyclopedia Britannica*. https://www.britannica.com/tropic/ARPANET

Federal Election Commission (2022, October). *Federal Election 2020*. FEC.gov. Retrieved February 20, 2023, from fec.gov/resources/cms-content/documents/federalelections2020.pdf

Ferguson C. J. (2013). Violent video games and the Supreme Court: lessons for the scientific community in the wake of Brown v. Entertainment Merchants Association. *The American psychologist, 68*(2), 57–74. https://doi.org/10.1037/a0030597

Figuls, J.C. (2023, May 26). Mark Coekelbergh: 'Weak democracies, capitalism, and artificial intelligence are a dangerous combination,' *EL PAIS English*. https://english.elpais.com/science-tech/2023-05-26/mark-coeckelbergh-weak-democracies-capitalism-and-artificial-intelligence-are-a-dangerous-combination.html

Flint, C.; & Taylor, P. J. (2018). Political Geography: world-economy, nation-state, and locality (7 ed.). Routledge. New York, NY.

Fischer, R. (2018. June 25). How Jim Morrison Predicted EDM to Rolling Stone in 1969. *Rolling Stone*. https://www.rollingstone.com/music/music-news/how-jim-morrison-predicted-edm-to-rolling-stone-in-1969-235437

Francis and Yazdinafard (2013). The Impact of Celebrity Endorsement and its Influence Through Different Scopes on the Retailing Business Across United States and Asia. *International Journal of Commerce, Business, and Management. Volume 2*(1), p.36 https://www.researchgate.net/publication/258511563_The_Impact_of_Celebrity_Endorsement_and_its_Influence_Through_Different_Scopes_on_the_Retailing_Business_Across_United_States_and_Asia

Forbes India (2024, January 2). *Top 10 People With Highest Followers on Instagram*. Retrieved January 12, 2024, from https://www.forbesindia.com/article/explainers/most-followed-instagram-accounts-world/85649/1

Forbes India (2024, January 31). *Top 10 most subscribed YouTube channels in the world [2024]*. Forbes India. https://www.forbesindia.com/article/explainers/most-subscribed-youtube-channels-in-the-world/87475/1

Frost, R. (1995). *Frost: Collected Poems, Prose, & Plays*. Library of America.

Fukuyama, F. (2006, March 1). *The End of History and the Last Man*. Free Press. New York, NY.

Galgut, E. (2019). Literary Form and Mentalization. *The Oxford Handbook of Philosophy and Psychoanalysis* (1st ed.). Oxford University Press. doi:10.1093/oxfordhb/9780198789703.013.30

Galston, W. A., & Kamarck, E. (2022, January 4). *Is democracy failing and putting our economic system at risk?* Brookings. https://www.brookings.edu/articles/is-democracy-failing-and-putting-our-economic-system-at-risk/

Game Industry News (2023, February 2). *The Top Ten Most Played Games Ever*. Retrieved February 15, 2023, from https://www.gameindustry.com/news-industry-happenings/the-top-10-most-played-games-ever/

Pepsico. (1991). *Like Mike* [Television Commercial]. National.

C.S. Mott Children's Hospital. (2020, January 20). *Game on: Teens and video games.* https://mottpoll.org/reports/game-teens-and-video-games

Gibbon, E. (1999). *History of the Decline and Fall of the Roman Empire Volume 1.* Wordsworth Editions.

Gibbs, S. (2017, December 29). *How did email grow from messages between academics to a global epidemic?* The Guardian. https://www.theguardian.com/technology/2016/mar/07/email-ray-tomlinson-history#:~:text=The%20very%20first%20version%20of,logging%20in%20from%20remote%20terminals

Golding, William, 1911-1993. (1954). Lord of the flies. New York: Perigee.

Grabow, C., & Rose, L. (2018, May 21). *The US has had 57 times as many school shootings as the other major industrialized nations combined.* CNN News. https://www.cnn.com/2018/05/21/us/school-shooting-us-versus-world-trnd/index.html

Granic, I., Lobel, A., & Engels, R. C. M. E. (2014). The benefits of playing video games. *American Psychologist, 69*(1), 66–78. https://doi.org/10.1037/a0034857

Greene, A. L. & Adams-Price, C., (1990), Adolescents' Secondary Attachments to Celebrity Figures, *Sex Roles,* 23 (7/8), 335-347.

Greenberg, D. (2024, February 20). Sports betting industry posts record $11B in 2023 revenue – ESPN. *ESPN.com.* https://www.espn.com/espn/betting/story/_/id/39563784/sports-betting-industry-posts-record-11b-2023-revenue

Hafford, M. (2017, March 24). Rolling Stone. *Rolling Stone.* https://www.rollingstone.com/feature/heavens-gate-20-years-later-10-things-you-didnt-know-114563/

Heilbroner, R. (1999). *The Worldly Philosophers.* Touchstone.

Hope, D. & Limberg, J. (2020) *The Economic Consequences of Major Tax Cuts for the Rich.* LSE International Inequalities Institute. https://eprints.lse.ac.uk/107919/1/Hope_economic_consequences_of_major_tax_cuts_published.pdf

Ivanovska, E. (2023, April 28). *America's Sports Watching Habits.* Time2play. Retrieved May 25, 2023, https://time2play.com/blog/americas-sports-watching-habits/

Jangid, Sanjay. (2022, April 7). *"The Significant Role of Art In Shaping Our Society."* Chitkara University, www.chitkara.edu.in/blogs/the-significant-role-of-art-in-shaping-our society/#:~:text=Artists%20provide%20creative%2C%20intellectual%20and,happier%20place%20to%20live%20in.

Juvenal. (2004) *Juvenal and Persius.* Harvard University Press. pp. 364-398.

Keller, J. (2022, June 9). *Keller @ Large: Are video games to blame for gun violence?* CBS News. https://www.cbsnews.com/boston/news/keller-large-are-video-games-to-blame-for-gun-violence/

Kemp, S. (2021, October 22). *Digital 2021 April StatShot Report — DataReportal – Global Digital Insights.* DataReportal – Global Digital Insights. https://datareportal.com/reports/digital-2021-april-global-statshot

Klepper, D., & Hinnant, L. (2021, December 17). *Far Right Using COVID-19 Theories to Grow Reach, Study Shows.* PBS News Hour. Retrieved January 25, 2023, from https://www.pbs.org/newshour/health/far-right-using-covid-19-theories-to-grow-reach-study-shows

"KRAFTON, INC. REPORTS $1.57 BILLION USD IN REVENUE FOR 2021, THE HIGHEST IN THE COMPANY'S HISTORY" (2022, October 2). *KRAFTON Press Room* https://press.krafton.com/KRAFTON-INC-REPORTS-157-BILLION-USD-IN-REVENUE-FOR-2021-THE-HIGHE

Lau, J.Y.F. (2024, February 26). Revisiting the origin of critical thinking. *Educational Philosophy and Theory*, 1-10.

Lincoln, A. (1953). *Collected Works of Abraham Lincoln, Volume 4 [Mar. 5, 1860 – Oct. 24, 1861].* Rutgers University Press.

Lee, I. (2013). *"Ragged Schools" (Discovering Literature: Romantics and Victorians, British Library, 2013).* British Library.

https://www.academia.edu/23052200/_Ragged_Schools_Discovering_Literature_Romantics_and_Victorians_British_Library_2013_

Lee, S., & Xenos, M. (2019). Social distraction? Social media use and political knowledge in two U.S. Presidential elections. *Computers in Human Behavior, 90,* 18–25. https://doi.org/10.1016/j.chb.2018.08.006

Levitsky, S., & Ziblatt, D. (2020). *The Crisis of American Democracy.* American Federation of Teachers. Retrieved April 25, 2023, from https://www.aft.org/ae/fall2020/levitsky_ziblatt

Levitsky, S., & Ziblatt, D. (2017, December 7). *How A Democracy Dies.* The New Republic. https://newrepublic.com/article/145916/democracy-dies-donald-trump-contempt-for-american-political-institutions

Logsdon, P.M. (2024. September 7). *Transcript of Dr. King Speech.* Ohio Northern University. https://www.onu.edu/mlk/mlk-speech-transcript

Lynch, J. (2007). *Becoming Shakespeare: The Unlikely Afterlife That Turned a Provincial Playwright into the Bard.* Walker Books.

MacDonald, K., & Stuart, K. (2021, June 24). *The 15 greatest video games of the 1990s – ranked!* The Guardian. https://www.theguardian.com/games/2021/jun/23/the-15-greatest-video-games-of-the-1990s-ranked

MacDonald, K., & Stuart, K. (2021, September 7*). The 15 greatest games of the 2010s – ranked!* The Guardian. https://www.theguardian.com/games/2021/sep/07/the-15-greatest-games-of-the-2010s-ranked

Massachusetts Institute of Technology. (2024, July 3). *Ray Tomlinson.* https://lemelson.mit.edu/reources/ray-tomlinson

Manoli, A. E. (2017, November 3). Sport marketing's past, present and future; an introduction to the special issue on contemporary issues in sports marketing. *Journal of Strategic Marketing, 26*(1), 1–5. tandfonline. https://doi.org/10.1080/0965254x.2018.1389492

Marlow, C. (1969). *Doctor Faustus.* Signet Classic.

Massey, A. (2015, April 24). *Your Imaginary Relationship With A Celebrity.* Pacific Standard. https://psmag.com/social-justice/rihanna-doesnt-give-a-crap-about-you

Maurer, J. (1999, March). *The History of Algorithmic Composition.* https://ccrma.stanford.edu/~blackrse/algorithm.html

Merriam-Webster. (2023). Information Age. In *Merriam-Webster.com dictionary.* Retrieved February 7, 2023 from https://www.merriam-webster.com/dictionary/Information%20Age

Merriam-Webster. (2023). Cult. In *Merriam-Webster.com dictionary*. Retrieved April 2, 2023 from https://www.merriam-webster.com/dictionary/cult

Merriam-Webster. (2023). Economics. In *Merriam-Webster.com dictionary*. Retrieved April 22, 2023 from https://www.merriam-webster.com/dictionary/economics

Merriam-Webster. (2024). Hegemony. In *Merriam-Webster Dictionary*. Retrieved July 6, 2023 https://www.merriam-webster.com/dictionary/hegemony

Merriam-Webster. (2024). Mercenary. In *Merriam-Webster.com dictionary*. Retrieved February 11, 2024 from https://www.merriam-webster.com/dictionary/mercenary

Merriam-Webster. (2024). Psychology. In *Merriam-Webster.com dictionary*. Retrieved February 2nd, 2024 from https://www.merriam-webster.com/dictionary/psychology

Meta Investor Relations. (2021, October 25). *Facebook reports third quarter 2021 results*. https://investor.fb.com/investor-news/press-release-details/2021/Facebook-Reports-Third-Quarter-2021-Results/default.aspx

Min, S. (2019, November 8). *86% of young Americans want to become a social media influencer*. CBS News. https://www.cbsnews.com/news/social-media-influencers-86-of-young-americans-want-to-become-one/

MIT. (2018, August 5). *MIT SHASS: At MIT Piketty calls for policies to reduce worldwide inequalities*. https://shass.mit.edu/news/mit-piketty-calls-policies-reduce-worldwide-inequalities

MLB.com (2024). *Pace of Play|Glossary|MLB.com*. MLB.com. https://www.mlb.com/glossary/rules/pace-of-play

Morin, R. (2002, February 2). *When celebrity endorsers go bad*. Washington Post. https://www.washingtonpost.com/archive/opinions/2002/02/03/when-celebrity-endorsers-go-bad/260776e6-d38c-4319-b683-eb466c499dce/

Nadworny, E. (2022, January 13). *More than 1 million fewer students are in college. Here's how that impacts the economy*. NPR. https://www.npr.org/2022/01/13/1072529477/more-than-1-million-fewer-students-are-in-college-the-lowest-enrollment-numbers-

National Science and Media Museum. (2020, December 3). *A short history of the internet | National Science and Media Museum*. National Science and Media Museum. https://www.scienceandmediamuseum.org.uk/objects-and-stories/short-history-internet

Nelson, S. A. (2014, June 9). *Why don't we talk anymore?* HuffPost. https://www.huffpost.com/entry/when-did-texting-replace_b_5105265

Nelson, T., Kagan, N., Critchlow, C., Hillard, A., & Hsu, A. (2020). The Danger of Misinformation in the COVID-19 Crisis. *Missouri medicine, 117*(6), 510–512.

Ngak, C. (2014, February 4). *Then and now: a history of social networking sites*. CBS News. https://www.cbsnews.com/pictures/then-and-now-a-history-of-social-networking-sites/5/

Nietzsche, F. (2005) *Thus Spoke Zarathustra*. New York, NY. Barnes and Noble Books.

NPR. (2012, May 21) How to get a celebrity endorsement from the Queen of England. *NPR*. https://www.npr.org/sections/money/2012/05/21/1531996

79/how-to-get-a-celebrity-endorsement-from-the-queen-of-england#:~:text=In%201765%2C%20for%20example%2C%20Wedwood,its%20elegance%20and%20aspirational%20qualities

Ong, D. (2023, July 10). *Richest Members of U.S. Congress: One is Worth almost Half a Billion*. International Business Times. https://www.ibtimes.com/richest-members-us-congress-one-worth-almost-half-billion-3704171

Orwell, G. (2021). *Nineteen eighty-four*. Penguin Classics. (Original work published 1949)

Oxford University Press. (2003). Education. In *Oxford American Dictionary and Thesaurus, p.458*. Oxford University Press.

Oxford English Dictionary. (2024). *Art*. In *OED.com dictionary*. Retrieved February 20, 2024 from *https://www.oed.com/search/dictionary/?scope=Entries&q=art&tl=true*

Paisley, L. (2016, November 8). *Political polarization at its worst since the Civil War*. USC Today. Retrieved February 3, 2023, from https://today.usc.edu/political-polarization-at-its-worst-since-the-civil-war-2/

Pallota, F. (2015, February 2). *Super Bowl XLIX Posts the Largest Audience in TV History*. CNN Money. https://money.cnn.com/2015/02/02/media/super-bowl-ratings/

Pelchen, L. (2024, March 1). Internet Usage Statistics in 2024. *Forbes Home*. https://www.forbes.com/home-improvement/internet/internet-statistics/#:~:text=There%20are%205.35%20billion%20internet%20users%20worldwide.&text=Out%20of%20the%20nearly%208,the%20internet%2C%20according%20to%20Statista

Pendlebury, T. (2022, January 12). *Making the next Beatles: How AI is changing pop music*. CNET. Retrieved February 12, 2023, from https://www.cnet.com/culture/entertainment/features/could-ai-create-a-future-grammy-award-winner-in-music/

Perkins, C. (2020, September 23). *A history of corruption in the United States*. Harvard Law Today. https://hls.harvard.edu/today/a-history-of-corruption-in-the-united-states/

Petrosyan, A. (2023, February 7). *Internet activities of U.S. users 2021*. https://www.statista.com/statistics/183910/internet-activities-of-us-users/

Phillips, B. (2002). *SparkNotes Lord of the Flies: William Golding*. Spark Publishing.

Pound, E. (1968). *Literary Essays*. New Directions.

Ray, J. (2021, January 15). *Gallup U.S. Global Leadership Update*. https://news.gallup.com/opinion/gallup/328490/gallup-global-leadership-update.aspx

Reed, B. (2022). *"The Guardian Views on the Book Publishing Industry: No One Size Fits All. The Guardian."* https://www.theguardian.com/commentisfree/2022/nov/04/the-guardian-view-on-the-book-publishing-industry-no-one-size-fits-all

Riehm, K. E., Mojtabai, R., Adams, L. B., Krueger, E. A., Mattingly, D. T., Nestadt, P. S., & Leventhal, A. M. (2021). Adolescents' Concerns About School Violence or Shootings and Association With Depressive, Anxiety, and Panic Symptoms. *JAMA network open, 4*(11), e2132131.

Rodgers, N. (2016). *The Illustrated Encyclopedia of the Roman Empire: Chronicling the Rise and Fall of the Most Important and Influential Civilization the World Has Ever Known.* Hermes House.

Rodriguez, S. (2021, December 14). *Instagram surpasses 2 billion monthly users while powering through a year of turmoil.* CNBC. https://www.cnbc.com/2021/12/14/instagram-surpasses-2-billion-monthly-users.html#:~:text=Instagram%20surpasses%202%20billion%20monthly%20users%20while%20powering%20through%20a%20year%20of%20turmoil&text=Instagram%20now%20has%20more%20than,knowledge%20of%20the%20key%20metric.

Roosevelt Institute. (2024). *The Franklin D. Roosevelt Presidential Library and Museum - Roosevelt Institute.* https://rooseveltinstitute.org/fdr-library/

Rose, J. (2022, January 3). *6 in 10 Americans say U.S. democracy is in crisis as the "Big Lie" takes root.* NPR. https://www.npr.org/2022/01/03/1069764164/american-democracy-poll-jan-6%20-%201/3/22

Santayana, G. (1905). The Life of Reason: p. 284 Vol. 1: *Reason of Common Sense.* London Constable.

Sawhney, T. (2018, June 29). *Gun fire every week – school shootings by the numbers.* The Clairemont Times. https://clairemonttimes.com/gun-fire-every-week-school-shootings-by-the-numbers/

Schiller, T. (2024, April 12). *Direct democracy.* Encyclopedia Britannica. http://www.britannica.com/topic/direct-democracy

Schoenherr, N. (2021, February 15). *What we don't understand about poverty in America.* The Source. Washington University in St. Louis. https://source.wustl.edu/2021/02/what-we-dont-understand-about-poverty-in-america/

Shakespeare, William. (1994) *William Shakespeare: The Complete Works.* Barnes and Noble, Inc.

Shapiro, A., Jarenwattananon, P., Restrepo, M. (2022, June 1). *In Britain, it took just one school shooting to pass major gun control.* NPR.org. Retrieved June 22, 2024, from https://www.npr.org/2022/06/01/1102239642/school-shooting-dunblane-massacre-uvalde-texas-gun-control

Sherman, A., & Morrissey, C. (2017). What Is Art Good For? The Socio-Epistemic Value of Art. *Frontiers in Human Neuroscience, 11*(411). https://doi.org/10.3389/fnhum.2017.00411

Shin, D. (2011) *Waxing the Korean Wave.* ARI Working Paper, 158, 1-21

Simpson, J. (2017, August 25). *Finding Brand Success In The Digital World.* Forbes. https://www.forbes.com/sites/forbesagencycouncil/2017/08/25/finding-brand-success-in-the-digital-world/?sh=42fe1164626e

Simpson, James (2023, 27 April). "Literary Traditions – Continuity and Change". *The Oxford History of Poetry in English: Volume 3. Medieval Poetry: 1400–1500.* Oxford University Press.

Smith, A. (1996). *Diversionary foreign policy in democratic systems.* International Studies Quarterly, *40*(1), 133-153. https://doi.org/10.2307/2600934

Spalding, R., & O'Donnell, C. (2020, December 31). U.S. vaccinations in 2020 fall far short of target of 20 million people. *Reuters.* https://www.reuters.com/article/us-health-coronavirus-usa-vaccinations/u-s-vaccinations-in-2020-fall-far-short-of-target-of-20-million-people-idUSKBN29512W

Statista Research Department. (2024, February 2). *Median Wealth per Member of U.S. Congress by Chamber 2008-2018.* https://www.statista.com/statistics/274581/median-wealth-per-member-of-us-congress-by-chamber/

Statista. (2022, November 28). *U.S. national school lunch program: federal costs FY 1996-2022.* https://www.statista.com/statistics/632322/us-national-school-lunch-program-federal-costs-timeline/

Stever, G.S. (2000). Parasocial and Social Interaction with Celebrities: Classification of Media Fans. *Journal of Media Psychology Theories Methods and Applications.* https://www.researchgate.net/publication/263258092_Parasocial_and_Social_Interaction_with_Celebrities_Classification_of_Media_Fans

Stone, O. (1987). *Wall Street.* Twentieth Century Fox.

Stuart, K. (2021, May 25). *The 15 greatest video games of the 70s – ranked!* The Guardian. https://www.theguardian.com/games/2021/may/13/15-greatest-video-games-of-the-70s-ranked

Stuart, K. (2021, May 27). *The 15 greatest video games of the 80s – ranked!* The Guardian. https://www.theguardian.com/games/2021/may/27/the-15-greatest-video-games-of-the-80s-ranked

Sullivan, B. (2023, September 22). *A Taylor Swift Instagram Post Helped Drive a Surge in Voter Registration.* NPR. https://www.npr.org/2023/09/22/1201183160/taylor-swift-instagram-voter-registration

Swatman, R. (2015). *1971: First Ever Email. Guinness World Records.* https://www.guinnessworldrecords.com/news/60at60/2015/8/1971-first-ever-email-392973#:~:text=Email%20began%20as%20an%20experiment,messages%20on%20machines%20for%20years

Suri, J. (2022, November 2). *The attack on Paul Pelosi and America's long history of political violence.* TIME. https://time.com/6227343/paul-pelosi-attack-political-violence-history/

The American Heritage dictionary of the English language. (2000). Boston: Houghton Mifflin.

The Britannica Dictionary. (2023). *Trickle–down Definition & Meaning.* Britannica Dictionary. https://www.britannica.com/dictionary/trickle%E2%80%93down#:~:text=TRICKLE%E2%80%93DOWN%20meaning%3A%20used%20to%20describe%20an%20economic%20theory,eventually%20help%20the%20poorer%20people%20in%20a%20society

The Editors of Encyclopedia Britannica. (2024, April 23), *Barbarian Invasions.* Encyclopedia Britannica. https://www.britannica.com/topic/barbarian-invasions

The Editors of Encyclopedia Britannica. (2024, June 22), *Roman Empire.* Encyclopedia Britannica. https://www.britannica.com/place/roman-empire

The Editors of Encyclopedia Britannica. (2024, June 17). *Columbine High School shootings.* Encyclopedia Britannica. https://www.britannica.com/event/Columbine-High-School-shootings

The Editors of Encyclopaedia Britannica. (2023, November 12). *Gettysburg Address.* Encyclopedia Britannica. https://www.britannica.com/event/Gettysburg-Address

The Editors of Encyclopaedia Britannica. (2023). *Gladiator | Roman sports*. In Encyclopædia Britannica. https://www.britannica.com/sports/gladiator

The Editors of Encyclopaedia Britannica. (2023, October 31). *Lemming | Definition, Size, Habitat, & Facts*. Encyclopedia Britannica. https://www.britannica.com/animal/lemming

The Federal Reserve. (2021) *"Table: Distribution of Household Wealth in the U.S. since 1989"*. www.federalreserve.gov. Retrieved February 4, 2023.

The Foundation for Critical thinking. (2023). *Defining critical thinking*. https://www.criticalthinking.org/pages/defining-critical-thinking/766

The Penguin Dictionary of Literary Terms and Literary Theory Fourth Edition KJ.A. Cuddon. (1999) Penguin Books. London, England

The United States Census Bureau (2023, January 29). *Population Clock World*. Retrieved February 17, 2023, from https://www.census.gov/popclock/world/in

Theiler, Tobias (2017, October 24). "The Microfoundations of Diversionary Conflict". *Security Studies*. 27 (2): 318–343. doi:10.1080/09636412.2017.138 6941. ISSN 0963-6412. S2CID 148629996.

Thomas, D. (1952). *The Poems of Dylan Thomas*. New Directions.

Tolstoy, L. (2000). *What is Art?* Replica Books. Bridgewater, NJ.

Tömmel, Tatjana, and Maurizio Passerin d'Entreves. "Hannah Arendt." *The Stanford Encyclopedia of Philosophy*. (Summer 2024 Edition). Edward N. Zalta and Uri Nodelman (eds.). http://plato.stanford.edu/entries/arendt/#Free NataPlur

Triana, Benjamin J. (2015). "Red Dead Masculinity: Constructing a Conceptual Framework for Analyzing the Narrative and Message Found in Video Games". *Journal of Games Criticism*. Rensselaer Polytechnic Institute. 2 (2). Archived from the original on October 12, 2015.

UNESCO. (2017.) *Re-Shaping Cultural Policies: Advancing Creativity for Development*. United Nations Educational, Scientific, and Cultural Organization. https://unesdoc.unesco.org/ark:/48223/pf0000260678

U.S. Department of Health and Human Services. (2022). *2022 Poverty Guidelines: 48 Contiguous States (all states except Alaska and Hawaii)*. https://aspe.hhs.gov/sites/default/files/documents/4b515876c46744664239 75826ac57583/Guidelines-2022.pdf

U.S. Const. (2012). *The Constitution of the United States of America with the Declaration of Independence*. Fall River Press.

Van Der Linden, S., Roozenbeek, J., & Compton, J. (2020). Inoculating against fake news about COVID-19. *Frontiers in Psychology, 11*. https://doi.org/10.33 89/fpsyg.2020.566790

Varga, Somogy and Charles Guignon, "Authenticity", The Stanford Encyclopedia of Philosophy (Summer 2023 Edition), Edward N. Zalta & Uri Nodelman (eds.), URL = <https://plato.stanford.edu/archives/sum2023/entries/authenticity/

Varnum, M. E. W., Krems, J. A., Morris, C., Wormley, A., & Grossmann, I. (2021). Why are song lyrics becoming simpler? a time series analysis of lyrical complexity in six decades of American popular music. *PloS one, 16*(1), e0244576. https://doi.org/10.1371/journal.pone.0244576

Washington Post. (2023). *data-school-shootings/school-shootings-data.csv at master-washingtonpost/data-school-shootings*. *GitHub*. https://github.com/washingtonpost/data-school-shootings/blob/master/school-shootings-data.csv#L116

Wagner, J. (2023, November 1). *How Much Money Do U.S. Lawmakers Make?* CBS News. https://www.cbsnews.com/minnesota/news/how-much-money-do-us-lawmakers-make/

Watts, E. J. (2020) *Mortal Republic: How Rome Fell into Tyranny*. Basic Books.

Weaver, Gary L. (1999) American Cultural Values, Kokusai Bunka Kenshu (Intercultural Training), *Special Edition*, pp 9-15 (reprinted for Interest-Based Negotiation Seminar, Air University, Maxwell AFB, AL 2 June 2006).

Weber, M. (2003) *The Protestant Ethic and the Spirit of Capitalism*. Garden City, NY. Dover Publications.

Worldometer (2023, February 7). *COVID-19 CORONAVIRUS PANDEMIC*. Worldometer.com. Retrieved February 7, 2023, from https://www.worldometers.info/coronavirus/

YourDictionary. (2024). Education. In *YourDictionary.com*. Retrieved February 11, 2024 from https://www.yourdictionary.com

Žižek, S. (2012, May 22). *Less Than Nothing: Hegel and the Shadow of Dialectical Materialism*. Verso Books, Brooklyn, NY.

Further Reading

Allen, K. & Twigg, K. (2021, March). *The disinformation tactics used by China.* BBC News. *https://www.bbc.com/news/56364952*

Bennett, Jessica (2021, September 1). "Monica Lewinsky Is (Reluctantly) Revisiting 'That Woman'". *The New York Times. ISSN 0362-4331. Retrieved January 20, 2023.*

Berkowitz, B., Lu, D., & Alcantara, C. (2021, December 1). *More Than 50 Years of Mass Shootings: The Victims, Sites, Killers and Weapons.* https://www.washingtonpost.com/graphics/2018/national/mass-shootings-in-america/

Bjelopera, J.P. Bagalman, E., Caldwell, S.W., Finklea, K.M. & McCallion, G. (2013, March 18) *Public Mass Shootings in the United States: Selected Implications for Federal Public Health and Safety Policy.* UNT Digital Library. https://digital.library.unt.edu/ark:/67531/metadc463383/

Bureau of Labor Statistics. *Department of Labor, The Economics Daily, Men spent 5.6 hours per day in leisure and sports activities, women 4.9 hours, in 2021 at* https://www.bls.gov/opub/ted/2022/men-spent-5-6-hours-per-day-in-leisure-and-sports-activities-women-4-9-hours-in-2021.htm *(visited February 8, 2023).*

Camus, A. (1955). *The Myth of Sisyphus.* Amereon Books. Mattituck, NY.

DiMaggio, P., Hargittai, E., Neuman, W. R., & Robinson, J. P. (2001). Social Implications of the Internet. *Annual Review of Sociology, 27,* 307–336. http://www.jstor.org/stable/2678624

Diomidous, M., Chardalias, K., Magita, A., Koutonias, P., Panagiotopoulou, P., & Mantas, J. (2016). Social and Psychological Effects of the Internet Use. *Acta informatica medica : AIM : journal of the Society for Medical Informatics of Bosnia & Herzegovina : casopis Drustva za medicinsku informatiku BiH, 24(1),* 66–68. *https://doi.org/10.5455/aim.2016.24.66-68*

Edosomwan, S., Prakasan, S. K., Kouame, D., Watson, J., & Seymour, T. (2011). The History of Social Media and Its Impact on Business. *Management, 16,* 79-91.

Firth, J., Torous, J., Stubbs, B., Firth, J. A., Steiner, G. Z., Smith, L., Alvarez-Jimenez, M., Gleeson, J., Vancampfort, D., Armitage, C. J., & Sarris, J. (2019). The "online brain": how the Internet may be changing our cognition. *World psychiatry: official journal of the World Psychiatric Association (WPA), 18(2),* 119–129. *https://doi.org/10.1002/wps.20617*

Follman, M., Aronson, G., & Pan, D. (December 6, 2023). US Mass Shootings, 1982–2023: Data From Mother Jones' Investigation. https://www.motherjones.com/politics/2012/12/ mass-shootings-mother-jones-full-data/

France: Samsung Electronics indicted for misleading advertising re. alleged labour abuses & child labour in China, S. Korea & Vietnam - Business & Human Rights Resource Centre. (n.d.). Business & Human Rights Resource Centre. https://www.business-humanrights.org/en/latest-news/france-samsung-electronics-indicted-for-misleading-advertising-re-alleged-labour-abuses-child-labour-in-china-s-korea-

vietnam/#:~:text=Samsung%20Electronics%20is%20facing%20charges,pare
nt%20company%20in%20South%20Korea

Grodzinski, A. (2015, December 14). *Do video games influence violent behavior?*
Michigan Youth Violence Preventions Center. https://yvpc.sph.umich.edu/
video-games-influence-violent-behavior/

Hernandez, F. A. (2021, June 4). *S.O.S.: Solar Observatory System; phase 1– a
lunar solar telescope in the south polar region.* University of Southern
California. https://news.usc.edu/4998/S-O-S-Solar-Observatory-System-ph
ase-1-a-lunar-solar-telescope-in-the-south-polar-region/

Kam, K. (2007, September 6). *4 Dangers of the internet. WebMD.* https://www.
webmd.com/parenting/features/4-dangers-internet

Kierkegaard, S. (2004). *Either/Or: A Fragment of Life.* Penguin Random House
UK.

Kroll, Justin (2020, February 13). *"'Crossfire' Movie Adaptation Lands at Sony
(EXCLUSIVE)". Variety.* Archived from the original on June 14, 2020. Retrieved
June 4, 2020.

Mass Shootings in America. (2018, September 13). Stanford Libraries. https://
library.stanford.edu/projects/mass-shootings-america

Mass Shooting Tracker. (n.d.). https://web.archive.org/web/20180104222719/
https://www.massshootingtracker.org/about

McGinty, J. C. (2021, February 19). The return on investment for 2021 Super
Bowl ads. *WSJ.* https://www.wsj.com/articles/the-return-on-investment-for-
2021-super-bowl-ads-11613730600

Moraes, M., Gountas, J., Gountas, S., & Sharma, P. (2019). Celebrity influences
on consumer decision making: new insights and research directions. *Journal
of Marketing Management, 35*(13–14), 1159–1192.

Mortality analyses - Johns Hopkins Coronavirus Resource Center. (March 16,
2023). Johns Hopkins Coronavirus Resource Center. https://coronavi
rus.jhu.edu/data/mortality

Mostafavi, B. (2020, January 20). *Healthier Video Game Habits: 5 Tips for Parents
of Teens.* Michigan Medicine. Retrieved January 28, 2023, from https://
www.michiganmedicine.org/health-lab/healthier-video-game-habits-5-tips
-parents-teens

Moyer, M. (2022, March 24). Kids as Young as 8 Are Using Social Media More
Than Ever, Study Finds. *The New York Times.* https://www.nytimes.com/
2022/03/24/well/family/child-social-media-use.html

Mueller, H. (2015, June 1) *The censorship of German video games: The effects of
national sensitivity ti violence in entertainment content.* https://scholars
bank.uoregon.edu/xmlui/handle/1974/19123#:~:text=Germany%20is%20on
e%20of%the,than%20the%20surrounding%20European%20nations.

Murray, M. (2022, September 27). *Poll: 61% of Republicans still believe Biden
didn't win fair and square in 2020.* NBC News. https://www.nbcnews.
com/meet-the-press/meetthepressblog/poll-61-republicans-still-believe-bi
den-didnt-win-fair-square-2020-rcna49630

Nakajima, K. (2021, July 14). *Database of mass killings and shootings in the US.
AP NEWS. https://projects.apnews.com/features/2023/mass-killings/index.
html*

Núñez-Gómez, P., Larrañaga, K. P., Rangel, C., & Ortega-Mohedano, F. (2021). Critical Analysis of the Risks in the Use of the Internet and Social Networks in Childhood and Adolescence. *Frontiers in psychology, 12*, 683384. https://doi.org/10.3389/fpsyg.2021.683384

Olivetti, Justin (2012, June 12). *"The Game Archaeologist: Maze War". Engadget. Yahoo. Archived from the original on May 6, 2018. Retrieved February 03, 2023.*

PBS. (2006). *The Roman Empire: in the First Century. The Roman Empire. Social Order: Plebians | PBS.* https://www.pbs.org/empires/romans/empire/plebians.html

Piketty, Thomas (2017). *Capital in the 21ˢᵗ Century.* Harvard University Press.

Randall, I. (2020, November 10). *Donald Trump uses Twitter to divert the media away from certain topics.* Mail Online. https://www.dailymail.co.uk/sciencetech/article-8932977/Trump-Study-reveals-President-uses-Twitter-divert-media-away-certain-topics.html

Rank, M. R., Eppard, L. M., & Bullock, H. E. (2021). *Poorly Understood: What America Gets Wrong About Poverty* (1st ed.). Oxford University Press.

Roosevelt Institute. (2023, August 8). *The Franklin D. Roosevelt Presidential Library and Museum - Roosevelt Institute.* https://rooseveltinstitute.org/fdr-library/#:~:text=%E2%80%9CDemocracy%20cannot%20succeed%20unless%20those,the%20schools%20in%20a%20democracy.%E2%80%9D

Samsung accused of "unsustainable labour practices" in its supply chain; Incl. co. statement - Business & Human Rights Resource Centre. (n.d.). Business & Human Rights Resource Centre. https://www.business-humanrights.org/en/latest-news/samsung-accused-of-unsustainable-labour-practices-in-its-supply-chain-incl-co-statement/

Sartre, J. P. (1988) *What is Literature? And Other Essays.* Harvard University Press. Cambridge, MA.

Shahrani, Sam (2006, April 5). "A History and Analysis of Level Design in 3D Computer Games". Gamasutra. UBM. Archived from the original on 2012-12-02.

Suciu, P. (2021, June 24). *Americans Spent On Average More Than 1,300 Hours On Social Media Last Year. Forbes.*https://www.forbes.com/sites/petersuciu/2021/06/24/americans-spent-more-than-1300-hours-on-social-media/?sh=39e272652547

Super Bowl Ratings History (1967-present). (February 8, 2019). Sports Media Watch. https://www.sportsmediawatch.com/super-bowl-ratings-historical-viewership-chart-cbs-nbc-fox-abc/

Tarawneh, R., MD. (2020, February 26). *How does the internet affect brain function?* The Ohio State University Wexner Medical Center. https://wexnermedical.osu.edu/blog/how-internet-affects-your-brain

The Editors of Encyclopedia Britannica. (2023, January 5). *Colosseum.* Encyclopedia Britannica. *https://www.britannica.com/topic/Colosseum*

The Editors of Encylopaedia Britannica. (2024, January 17). *Hegemony | Definition, Theory, & Facts.* Encyclopedia Britannica. https://www.britannica.com/topic/hegemony

The Editors of Encyclopedia Britannica. (2023, November 3). *Idolatry |
   Definition, History & Types*. Encyclopedia Britannica. https://www.brita
   nnica.com/topic/idolatry

Varrall, Merridan (2020, January 16). *"Behind the News: Inside China Global
   Television Network"*. Lowy Institute. Archived from the original on 26 July
   2020. Retrieved 11 May 2020.

"World population estimates and UN projection". Our World in Data. Retrieved
   1 November 2021. – The United Nations

Žižek,S. (2009). *The Sublime Object of Ideology*. Verso Books.

Short Statement on the History of the Development of the Book

This book grew out of a need for it. Roman history intersects with modern history in many places. Juvenal's writings are a great point of intersection to begin examination. No parts of this book draw from previously published material by the author. The book was written out of a zeal for writing and a passion for doing everything in my power to attempt to call attention to a problem and present solutions to that problem in order to redeem and ameliorate society, which is a vital role literature has played throughout human history. In doing so, the book's development was aimed at improving my relationship with my fellow human being and, more importantly, at improving my fellow human being's relationship with each other.

Kurt Warner

Index

www.ingramcontent.com/pod-product-compliance
Lightning Source LLC
Chambersburg PA
CBHW050519280326
41932CB00014B/2387